I0016520

Displacement Mapping and Volume Rendering Graphics Hardware

by
Michael C. Doggett

ISBN: 1-58112-166-0

DISSERTATION.COM

USA • 2002

Displacement Mapping and Volume Rendering Graphics Hardware

Copyright © 2001 Michael C. Doggett
All rights reserved.

Dissertation.com
USA • 2002

ISBN: 1-58112-166-0

www.dissertation.com/library/1121660a.htm

Displacement Mapping
and
Volume Rendering
Graphics Hardware

Michael Doggett
Tübingen
2001

The work documented in this dissertation was done at the GRaphisch-Interaktive Systeme (Computer Graphics Laboratory) in the Wilhelm Schickard Institut für Informatik, Universität Tübingen from March 1998 to January 2001 towards the German degree of Habilitation under the supervision of Prof. Dr.-Ing Wolfgang Straßer.

Abstract

This dissertation introduces new hardware architectures for more realistic surface rendering of three dimensional objects and the rendering of volumetric datasets. Surface rendering is dealt with in the first part of the dissertation where the architectures for displacement map rendering in hardware are proposed. This work represents the first to appear in scientific literature on displacement map hardware rendering. Where possible these architectures propose components that integrate into currently available pipelines and make use of existing units in those pipelines. Displacement map rendering in hardware is a desired feature currently under development by most graphics hardware vendors. The first architecture is scan-line based and works just before rasterization and the second adaptively retessellates a triangle mesh using additional hardware on either side of the geometry transformation stage in the graphics pipeline.

The VIZARDII architecture and several hardware based performance improvements for any ray casting architecture are presented in the second part titled Volume Rendering. VIZARDII is an interactve programmable hardware acelerator for Volume Rendering implemented on a PCI Card. The main pipeline is implemented on a Xilinx FPGA allowing new features to be added relatively quickly. A memory interface is presented and discussed with its final implementation appearing in the VIZARDII system. Novel architectures for ray queuing and sorting, sub-cube based space leaping are also presented which improve the performance of ray casting based hardware architectures. Antialiasing that occurs when ray casting volume data is also discussed and possible solutions are presented using multiresolution volume datasets.

Acknowledgements

Thanks to Professor Strasser for inviting me to Tübingen to further my research in Volume Rendering hardware with the GRIS research lab. I am also thank him for his wisdom and guidance during my time here. Thanks to Andreas Schilling for his brilliant insights into my work, willingness to help and associated suggestions.

Thanks to Johannes Hirche, Anders Kugler, Michael Meißner, Urs Kanus, Dirk Bartz, Gregor Wetekam, Olaf Etzmuß, Rainer Jäger, Helga Mayer, Edelhard Becker and all the members of the GRIS lab that have made my time at GRIS both rewarding and enjoyable.

Thanks to Roland Proksa, and our partners at Philips Research Laboratories in Hamburg for our work together on the VIZARDII and DynCT projects.

Parts of this work were funded by the Commission of the European Communites (CEC) and the SFB grant 382 of the German Research Council (DFG).

Thanks to Gaby, Iliana and Cassandra for always being there for me.

Contents

List of Figures

List of Tables

1

Chapter 1

Introduction

While the amount of photorealism in real-time rendering systems has increased to an impressive level in recent years, the demand for even more realistic images has not subsided. To meet these demands the feature lists for currently available three dimensional graphics cards has grown to include techniques such as bump mapping. This dissertation presents novel work into the next step in fulfilling this ever increasing demand in the form of hardware based displacement map rendering.

Along with these demands for photorealism is the growing interest in real-time visualization of volume data. Several novel architectures to improve the performance of these visualization systems in general are presented along with the architecture of the VIZARDII system.

1.1 Overview

This dissertation starts with a brief overview of graphics hardware starting with the basic concepts used in surface rendering including displacement mapping in Chapter 2. Chapter 2 also presents the fundamental algorithms used for Volume Rendering using ray casting and some previous hardware architectures.

The dissertation is then broken into two parts. The first presents two approaches to displacement mapping in hardware. Chapter 3 presents a scan line based approach where triangles are processed in screen space and a new displaced mesh generated and rendered. This work was first presented in [18] and the final version on which the chapter will be published in a journal next year[19].

Chapter 4 presents a different approach to displacement mapping hardware

3

that takes advantage of geometry engines which are becoming common in PC based graphics hardware. This work was first presented in sketch form[17]with a final full paper on which the chapter is based appearing in[16]. Further work following on from the adaptive architecture for rendering of subdivision surfaces is presented in [2].

The second part of the dissertation deals with Volume Rendering and in particular ray casting hardware architectures. Chapter 5 presents a low-cost memory interface that takes advantage of SDRAM technology and removable Dual Inline Memory Modules (DIMMs). This work was first presented in [20] and the final version on which the chapter is based is presented in in [21]. To further improve the performance of ray casting based Volume Rendering a ray queueing and sorting design is described in Chapter 6 which is based on the work from [15]. Ray casting is can be further improved by avoiding the wasting of cycles on empty space and a design to achieve this improvement is presented in Chapter 7 based on work that will be published in [62].

Chapter 8 presents some of the problems encountered by ray casting algorithms in general that can appear as aliasing artifacts. Proposals to solve this problem are presented in the chapter which is based on work from [22].

The VIZARDII interactive volume rendering system is presented in Chapter 9. This ray casting, image-order based hardware accelerator imploys the memory interface from Chapter 5 and the ray queueing from Chapter 6 into a fully featured PCI Card for interactive Volume Rendering.

Chapter 2

Graphics Hardware

Graphics Hardware includes the algorithms, systems, electronic computational and storage devices that are reponsible for digital image synthesis on modern computer systems. The design that places many digital devices, from the system level down to the gate level elaborating a hierarchy of structure and order is often referred to as the *Architecture*. The objective of graphics hardware architectures over the last 15 years has been to find a careful balance between performance and features in what has become one of the most competitive markets in the computing industry today. It is this architectural design from top level issues such as parallelisation right down to low level issues of high performance arithmetic operations that determines whether the computer user can let go of their real world and become totally immersed inside the world generated inside the computer.

3D graphics architectures have focused on the rendering of triangles which are used to model objects in three dimensions. But three dimensional objects can be represented using a large range of representations. The basic representation of objects in three dimensional space used has determined many of the approches to architectural design over the last 15 years, but now new methods of object representation and their sampling for image rendering are being investigated leading to a profond influence on the way graphics architectures will be designed in the future. Currently systems capable of rendering millions of flat shaded triangles per second are readily available resulting in a focus shift away from performance towards features and high quality rendering[36].

We can categorise graphics hardware architectures based on the fundamental type of geometric primitive they use to generate 2D images. This dissertation deals the two most common types of representation, surface and volume based systems. While surface rendering has traditionally been driven by triangle render-

5

ing pipelines, higher order primitives are of increasing importance and the rendering of these primitives in hardware is expected this year. Also with the advent of new concepts of the image synthesise process completely new approaches to architectural design become possible marking the beginning of a whole new era in Graphics Hardware design and research.

2.1 Surface Rendering

Standard rendering hardware contains a rasteriser that scan converts triangles or polygons into pixels and then sends the pixels to the output display. Traditional shaded triangle scan conversion is typically performed by a pipeline of an edge-walking phase followed by the span interpolation. An edge processor decomposes triangles into horizontal spans. Spans are further decomposed into pixels by a span processor. Span interpolation forms the inner loop of the triangle shading pipeline; it interpolates the colour, depth, texture coordinate and normal vector along the current span. During edge interpolation, a triangle is scanned horizontally from top to bottom, delivering the boundaries of the triangle, the starting and ending values of texture coordinates, (u, v, w), normal, (N_x, N_y, N_z), colour (R, G, B), and depth, Z, for the span interpolation. The span processor generates one pixel per cycle in the X-direction. Alternatives to scan-line rasterisation such as stamp based rasterisation are also used for rasterization[61, 60].

2.1.1 Texture and Bump Mapping

Texture and bump mapping are rendering techniques for adding more surface detail to computer-generated objects. Today's standard for texture filtering is mipmapping[89], where textures are stored according to their level of detail.

Bump mapping, introduced by Blinn[5], perturbs surface normals on a surface as if a height field displaced the surface in the direction of the original surface normal. Bump mapping does not change the underlying geometry of the model, but fools the shading to produce an interesting surface. Since bump mapping only changes the appearance of an object, it makes certain approximations. Standard techniques for bump mapping assume that the bumpiness is only microdisplacements and hence assume the magnitude of the height field is negligible. Blinn[5] presented two methods for computing bump mapping the first used Offset Vector bump maps and the second Vector Rotation bump maps.

Bump mapping is applied to a surface by taking the surface normal vector $\hat{\mathbf{N}}$ at a point $\mathbf{P}$ which is perturbed by a perturbation vector $\mathbf{B}$ dependent on a perturbation function $\mathbf{F}(u, v)$ of the surface parameters, stored as a two-dimensional table indexed by the texture coordinate (u, v). For a point $\mathbf{P}$ on a surface $\mathbf{S}(u, v)$, the normal vector $\mathbf{N}$ at that point is expressed as:

$$\mathbf{N}_p = \mathbf{S}_u \times \mathbf{S}_v = \frac{\partial \mathbf{S}}{\partial u} \times \frac{\partial \mathbf{S}}{\partial v} \tag{2.1}$$

where $\mathbf{S}_u$ and $\mathbf{S}_v$ are the partial derivatives in the parameter directions u, v. The new normal to the perturbed surface is given by:

$$\mathbf{N}' = \mathbf{N} + \underbrace{\frac{\mathbf{F}_u(\mathbf{N} \times \mathbf{S}_v)}{|\mathbf{N}|} + \frac{\mathbf{F}_v(bf S_u \times \mathbf{N})}{|\mathbf{N}|}}_{\mathbf{B}'} \tag{2.2}$$

Since bump mapping modifies the original normal vectors it requires the normal vector to be interpolated across the current triangle. Different types of hardware architectures were described in the past for texture and bump mapping support [25, 71, 50].

Bump mapping requires interpolating the Cartesian coordinates of surface normals and applying the perturbation in a local coordinate system $\mathbf{E}_u, \mathbf{E}_v, \mathbf{E}_w$ tangent to the surface, defined by the normalised surface normal vector $\hat{\mathbf{N}}$ and two vectors perpendicular to $\hat{\mathbf{N}}$. A local and orthonormal coordinate system can be built from the interpolated surface normal $\mathbf{N}$ and a constant main direction $\mathbf{M}$, such as the polar axis, as shown by Schilling [79] :

$$\mathbf{E}_w = \frac{\mathbf{N}}{||\mathbf{N}||} = \hat{\mathbf{N}} \quad \mathbf{E}_u = \frac{\mathbf{M} \times \mathbf{N}}{||\mathbf{M} \times \mathbf{N}||} \quad \mathbf{E}_v = \mathbf{E}_w \times \mathbf{E}_u \tag{2.3}$$

$$\mathbf{A} = [\mathbf{E}_u \mathbf{E}_v \mathbf{E}_w]^{\mathbf{T}} \tag{2.4}$$

and the new normal $\mathbf{N}'$ to the surface becomes:

$$\mathbf{N}' = \mathbf{N} + \mathbf{A}\mathbf{B} \tag{2.5}$$

Bump mapping best approximates an embossed surface when the heights of the bumps are not too great and when the surface is viewed from a direction close to the surface normal. When looking at a rendered object, bump mapping can be recognised immediately, in the sense that the bumps do not "pop out"of the surface at silhouettes or edges.

Several hardware based approaches to implementing bump mapping have been presented in recent years[25, 71, 50]. Peercy[71] presents an implementation for high-end 3D graphics hardware that supports bump mapping within the context of per-fragment lighting operations. Kilgard[42] presents an approach to bump mapping that takes advantage of currently available low-cost graphics hardware.

The limitation of bump mapping becomes obvious when the surface is parallel to the viewer and the bump does not create a silhouette. Also as a surface moves in perspective space the shape created in the viewers mind by the bump map will not occlude other objects. Bump mapping can only simulate the roughness of natural surfaces with only small deformations well, it cannot be used to alter the geometry of a surface. To alter the geometry of the surface displacement mapping is needed.

2.1.2   Displacement Mapping

To add real geometric detail to a flat surface, *displacement mapping,* first introduced by Cook[10], can be used.

Displacement mapping uses a base surface defined by a bivariate vector function $\mathbf{P}(u,v)$[1] that defines 3D points (x,y,z) on the surface. Displacement values for the surface of the object are determined from the displacement map in a similar fashion to determining the colours of a surface from a texture map. The displacements from the surface are defined by a bivariate scalar function $d(u,v)$ and the normals on the base surface $\mathbf{P}(u,v)$ by $\hat{\mathbf{N}}(u,v)$. The points on the new displaced surface $\mathbf{P}'(u,v)$ are defined as follows:

$$\mathbf{P}'(u,v) = \mathbf{P}(u,v) + d(u,v)\hat{\mathbf{N}}(u,v) \tag{2.6}$$

where $\hat{\mathbf{N}}(u,v) = \frac{\mathbf{N}(u,v)}{|\mathbf{N}(u,v)|}$.

A cross section of an example displacement mapped surface is shown in Figure 2.1, where $\mathbf{N}'(u,v)$ is the normal to the displaced surface.

As an example Figure 2.2(a) shows a flat plane with a colour texture applied, which is displaced using the displacement map in Figure 2.2(b), where white represents a high displacement and black represents no displacement. The application of the displacement map to the plane results in the the displaced surface shown in Figure 2.2(c).

---

[1]A bivariate vector function is a function of two variables where the result is a vector.

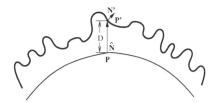

Figure 2.1: A cross section of a displaced surface.

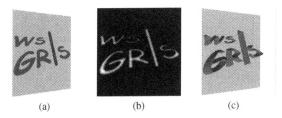

(a)   (b)   (c)

Figure 2.2: A plane displaced with a text displacement map.

The obvious method to alter surface geometry would be to alter the vertices of a triangle mesh representing a surface as presented above and then rerender the triangle mesh every frame. This is a very expensive operation for the processor and is only accurate at the mesh vertices.

Displacement mapping is also an effective technique for encoding the high levels of detail found in today's triangle based surface models such as those generated by 3D scanning technologies. A coarse approximation of a surface can be modeled with a triangle mesh that is sent to the graphics processor with more detail added to the surface by rendering it with displacement mapping. Also once the displacement map is transferred to the graphics processor memory it can be reused across a surface several times and by multiple surfaces.

A common bottleneck for modern 3D PC graphics cards is the transfer of triangle vertex data from the CPU to the graphics processor. The drawback to performing displacement mapping in hardware would be that it moves the bottleneck to the graphics processor which must now process an increased number of triangles. But adding displacement map rendering into graphics rendering pipeline presents several problems. So far these have been virtually no approaches to displacement mapping hardware presented in literature.

But, a large amount of work exists on the use of displacement mapping in software based photorealistic rendering systems.

Miyata [64] uses a height map as one parameter for the generation of highly realistic stone wall patterns. Witkin and Kass [90] present a method for texture synthesis based on the simulation of a process of local nonlinear interaction, called reaction-diffusion and apply this texture synthesis to texture and displacement mapping techniques. Cohen and Shaked [9] present a method for the generation of photo-realistic images of views over terrain datasets by mapping a digital aerial photograph on a perspective projection of a digital elevation map. Pedersen [70] extended the notion of displacement mapping by allowing displacements to be defined along curved trajectories of flow fields effectively extending the class of shapes that can be modeled using displacement maps. Krishnamurthy[48] uses displacement maps that specify the vector direction in which displacement occurs allowing more complex objects to be represented. These techniques typically use a parametrically described curved surface, which is displaced, and then tessellated and rendered as a set of triangles. This means that if the displacement map is changed and the surface is changed accordingly, then a new tessellation is required making none of these approaches practical for real-time rendering.

Pharr[74] presents a geometry cache to allow displacement mapping to be used in a ray-tracing renderer. The cache is used to handle the large amount of geometry that is generated by displacement mapping and make it available by rendering the image in a coherent manner and taking advantage of the fact that rays are spatially coherent. In [80], Sprites with Depth are presented as a new image based primitive for image-based rendering. This primitive is used in a similar fashion to displacement mapping. Sprites with Depth could also be used as a primitive for hardware acceleration, but rendering subsequent images from the primitive places heavy restrictions on the available viewpoints. Schuafler[78] presents an algorithm for rendering displacements maps using image warping at interactive rates. A compact surface representation using scalar-valued displacements over a smooth domain surface is presented by Lee[53].

Terrain modelling using height fields is closely related to the rendering of displacement maps since height fields are identical in concept to displacement maps. Many algorithms are available for approximating terrains and height fields using polygonal meshes. These algorithms approximate the height field with a mesh of triangles, also known as a triangulated irregular network, or TIN. Garland et al.[30] analyses several of these algorithms including the greedy insertion algorithm. They present a refinement of the greedy insertion algorithm that inserts the point with the greatest error from the current approximation after every pass over the current mesh. While very good results are achieved these techniques relie on global mesh information making hardware implementation expensive.

2.1.3 Higher Order Primitive Rendering

The next step in surface modeling is the use of higher order primitives instead of triangles. Rockwood et al. [77] present a technique for Real-Time rendering of trimmed surfaces including NURBs that is modular and can be balanced for different hardware implementations. They first convert all surfaces into Bezier patches. They are then subdivided into uv-monotone regions and tessellated into a grid of rectangular *tiles* trimmed by triangular *coving*. The tile size is computed on a per patch basis by transforming the control mesh of the patch into screen space. Step sizes in u and v directions are determined that guarantee the size of the tiles, when projected to screen space, will be smaller than a user specified tolerance. Rockwood's method has the following steps: Convert to Bezier Patches; Calculate Step Sizes; Find Extrema; Divide into uv-monotone Regions; Cove and Tile; Evaluate Surface Functions; Render Facets. They compute the normal vector by evaluating the partial derivatives of the surface in the u and v directions, taking their cross project and normalizing the result. This scheme is the tessellation scheme used in the GLU extensions to OpenGL.

Vlachos[83] introduces an N-Patch which is an interpolating Triangluar Cubic Bezier Surface. A 10-point control mesh is needed to tessellate this surface. The control mesh is derived from three point/normal pairs (a triangle). Six points, called boundar points (not necessarily on the boundary) are derived. An interior control point is calculated from the other nine control points (three original vertices and the six border points). An integer tessellation level is specified and then the final tessellated triangles are passed off to the programmable vertex shader.

2.2 Volume Rendering

Visualization of volumetric datasets is driven by the need to reach a better understanding and insight of measured or computed data. Many scientific and increasingly everyday applications require this insight, including areas in medicine, geophysics, scientific simulations and industry. The user gains greater insight and understanding with higher accuracy, perspective images, and direct control over the image synthesis process.

Two dimensional images can be generated from three dimensional volume datasets using either indirect or direct Volume Rendering. Indirect Volume Rendering involves transforming the dataset into another representation, such as triangles in the case of the Marching Cubes algorithm[58]. A triangle representation can then be easily rendered in real-time using modern 3D graphics hardware, but only specified iso-values are represented and a change in these values results in a non-interactive pre-processing stage. The rendering of semi-transparent iso-surfaces is also a difficult problem at interactive frame-rates since it requires depth sorting of all triangles prior to rendering. Direct Volume Rendering involves generating final pixel values by compositing together filtered samples of the original voxel values. In order to achieve interactive frame-rates this approach can be implemented in software, using readily available graphics hardware, or special purpose hardware.

One of the most popular methods for Direct Volume Rendering is ray casting. Ray casting was presented by Levoy[54] and is capable of generating high quality images from Volume data. Ray casting involves tracing one ray for each pixel from a viewing point through a view plane (or screen) and into the 3D dataset as shown in Figure 2.3. As the ray travels through the dataset sample values are trilinearly interpolated from the surrounding data at predetermined intervals. Each sample value is calculated from the eight voxels that form a cube surrounding the sample point. These samples values are classified and a gradient calculated. Classification is the process of looking up from a table of user defined values, colour, opacity and possibly other values for each interpolated sample. Using the results from classification and the gradient calculated at the sample point, shading is calculated as if a surface were present and shaded samples are composited together with the other shaded samples along the same ray. The composited shaded values along the ray make up one pixel on the screen. The process is then repeated for each pixel in the view plane.

Distance coding is a technique to improve the performance of ray casting by storing at each voxel the distance of empty space surrounding it. When this voxel is read a distance value is also read and traversal along the ray can increment by the distance instead of by a smaller step. Distance coding introduces a hazard for hardware based pipelined implementations because the position of the next voxel along a ray requires the distance from the previous step to have been already read from memory and added.

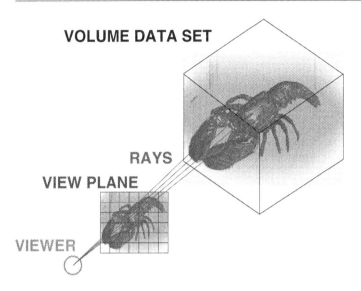

Figure 2.3: The viewer, viewplane and Volume dataset as used in Ray Casting.

Shear-Warp[51] is recognized as the fastest software renderer to date and uses an image and three run length encoded data sets. For datasets and classifications where the volume can be encoded efficiently, interactive frame-rates can be achieved. However, interpolation is only bilinear, the encoding scheme requires significant pre-processing time (making interactive changes to the classification cumbersome), and for semi-transparent rendering, the overall performance drops significantly.

2D and 3D Texture Mapping hardware can also be used for Volume Rendering using a variety of techniques. By resampling a 3D texture map using texture mapped planes parallel to the view plane [12], interactive frame-rates can be achieved on the SGI Reality Engine [8]. Texture Mapping illumination limitations can be overcome by storing gradients for iso-surfaces allowing for illumination calculations to be performed with pixel textures [85]. This can be extended to allow for changes in classification and multiple classification spaces[67]. Low cost Volume Rendering has also become available recently on PC graphics cards using 2D Texture Mapping [76], and 3D Texture Mapping [3]. However, Texture Mapping hardware has several general limitations including, no gradient calculation, no specular illumination, limited arithmetic precision for blending and interpolation, and no opacity correction to handle perspective rendering correctly.

Doggett[24, 14, 23] presented VIZAR, one of the first truly hybrid image-order hardware renderers with an object-order memory accessing scheme to the Volume data. This design was scalable and capable of a few frames per second using the technology available at that time, but was never realised.

Knittel[45, 46] presented VIZARD, the first PCI-based true ray casting Volume Rendering accelerator capable of providing a few frames per second for 256^3 datasets. The PCI based accelerator uses the host main memory to store the volume data and utilizes FPGAs. Before rendering, the data is pre-shaded and compressed in software using a lossy compression scheme. The system is limited by the inability to change classification and shading. This is due to the pre-processing stage and the use of main memory to store the volume dataset, resulting in the performance being severely restricted by the PCI bus.

One of the early proposals to Volume Rendering hardware was presented by Kaufman et al.[41]. Using parallel operating pipelines – each containing one memory unit – the memory requirements are reduced by exchanging data locally between pipelines. Furthermore, a skewing scheme is used to guarantee a conflict-free access to any axis-parallel beam of voxels. While this scheme aggravates the integration of features like multiple classification spaces or over-sampling of the viewplane, a high memory bandwidth can be accomplished enabling real-time volume rendering[73, 40]. However, the Cube architectures are more of an object space approach simulating ray-casting by limiting the process to parallel projections, than a true ray-casting accelerator providing perspective projections and requiring random access. The EM-Cube architecture [69] works on the assumption that all voxels are read from memory to generate one image so that modern memory burst mode reading of sub-cubes or blocks can be used, the final implementation of which appears in VolumePro.

VolumePro [72] delivers insight and control over the rendering process of a volume dataset unlike any previously available solution to Real-Time Volume Rendering. VolumePro's performance is due to its architecture[2] and the use of ASIC technology, providing unprecedented frame-rates. The scalable parallel

---

[2]The architecture is based mainly on the Shear-Warp approach.

pipelines in the VolumePro architecture relies on the availability of neighboring voxels in the pipeline which means that the generation of perspective images as well as the use of arbitrary sampling distances is not feasible or requires multi-pass approaches. Furthermore, reprogramming of the feature set, or algorithmic speed-ups are generally not possible without a costly and time consuming redesign of the ASIC.

Many more proposals for Volume Rendering hardware architectures also exist[44, 33, 57, 56, 4, 47].

Part I

Displacement Mapping

Chapter 3

A Scan Conversion Hardware Architecture

This chapter presents a novel algorithm and architectures for perspective correct displacement of the surface geometry of a polygonal model using a displacement map. This new displaced surface geometry is passed onto a traditional rendering pipeline. The algorithm uses a multiple pass approach in which the geometry is displaced in the first pass and then the displaced geometry is rendered. The significant features of the algorithm are that the surface is displaced after its triangle mesh is transformed into screen space and that it uses only bilinear interpolation for calculating the displaced geometry allowing a cheap incremental scan-line implementation. A hardware architecture based on this algorithm is presented along with possible alternative implementations.

The algorithm presented here uses two passes, in the first pass the displacement map is used to calculate new screen coordinates for the triangles generated by a scan conversion of the original triangle mesh. The method presented here does not alter the geometry of the original surface, but calculates detailed geometry without having to specify and transform a hugely complex mesh. Original triangles are scanned on a coarser grid than the screen pixel grid resulting in an approximation of the displaced surface and a number of triangles that can be handled by the render pipeline.

Independent work on displacement mapping hardware[32] represents a series of algorithms optimized for hardware implementation. In comparison the technique presented in this chapter reuses the standard scan conversion pipeline and adds only small additional computational units to perform displacement mapping. In [32], a 3rd dimension for scan conversion and a multi-resolution griding system

19

Coordinate System	Definition	Other Names	Notation
Model	Individual objects are defined.	object-coordinate or object-definition space	
World	A consistent universe into which all modeled objects are placed.	homogeneous space before perspective	$(E_x, E_y, E_z, 1)$
Eye	Where a scene or complete object is represented in the computer and objects are transformed into. Space after the perspective transform.	camera-coordinate system or homogeneous space after perspective	$(\tilde{P}_x, \tilde{P}_y, \tilde{P}_z, \tilde{P}_w)$
Post-perspective	Distorted space after perspective division by the homogeneous coordinate.		$(P_x, P_y, P_z, 1)$
3D screen	X, Y, Z coordinates in the hardware pixel space.	3D normalised or logical device coordinates	(x, y, z)

Table 3.1: Coordinate System Terminology.

are introduced requiring substantial additional calculations per triangle and hence a much larger implementation than the architectures presented here.

Coordinate System Terminology

The terminology used in this chapter for coordinate systems is shown in Table 3.1. The Coordinate System definitions used are taken from[29]. We assume that the eye-coordinate system is normalised to the device coordinates. The eye-coordinate system uses homogeneous coordinates and the perspective division has not been performed. Eye space is considered analogous to perspective space. The last coordinate system, the 2D device coordinate system, normalised device-coordinate system or image-coordinate system, will not generally be referred to here even though it is the coordinate system for the frame-buffer. We assume that the 3D screen coordinates have been normalised to the logical device coordinates.

3.1 Scan Conversion Displacement Mapping Algorithm

To integrate displacement mapping into a standard hardware rendering pipeline a new approach to displacement mapping is required which is described in this section.

Displacement mapping starts with a surface tessellated with triangles, and each triangle of the surface has a (u, v)-texture parameterisation. The texture coordinate (u, v) is used to index into a height field table or displacement map. The corresponding position on the surface is then displaced along the normal by an offset read from a displacement map at that position on the surface.

This algorithm allows displacement mapping to be accomplished using standard rasterisation pipelines without needing to recalculate a displaced surface before rendering. The principal idea is to scan convert the triangle and interpolate it's corresponding maximally displaced triangle. Figure 3.1 shows a pixel on one scan line of a triangle with the maximally displaced pixel and the displaced pixel interpolated between the two. The interpolation of the pixel position on the base triangle is performed by the scan conversion in screen space. The maximally displaced pixel is then bilinearly interpolated in eye space and the final displaced pixel position is interpolated in eye space and transformed back to screen space.

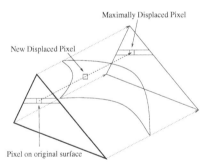

Figure 3.1: The pixel, its maximally displaced position and its new position on the displaced surface.

Vertex data	Coordinate System	
Vertex coordinates	World	$\mathbf{V} = (E_x, E_y, E_z, 1)$
Vertex coordinates	Perspective eye	$\tilde{\mathbf{V}} = (\tilde{V}_x, \tilde{V}_y, \tilde{V}_z, \tilde{V}_w)$
Vertex coordinates	Post-perspective	$\mathbf{V} = (\tilde{V}_x/\tilde{V}_w, \tilde{V}_y/\tilde{V}_w, \tilde{V}_z/\tilde{V}_w, 1)$
Maximum displaced vertex	Perspective eye	$\tilde{\mathbf{V}}_\mathbf{m} = (\tilde{V}_{mx}, \tilde{V}_{my}, \tilde{V}_{mz}, \tilde{V}_{mw})$
Texture coordinates	-	(U, V)
Texture coordinates	-	$(u, v, q) = (U/\tilde{V}_w, V/\tilde{V}_w, 1/\tilde{V}_w)$
Perspective coordinate	3D screen	$q = 1/\tilde{V}_w$
Span generation data	Coordinate System	
Pixel coordinates	3D screen	$\mathbf{S} = (x, y, z)$
Pixel coordinates	Perspective eye	$\tilde{\mathbf{P}} = (\tilde{P}_x, \tilde{P}_y, \tilde{P}_z, \tilde{P}_w)$
Maximum displaced pixel coordinates	Perspective eye	$\tilde{\mathbf{P}}_\mathbf{m} = (\tilde{P}_{mx}, \tilde{P}_{my}, \tilde{P}_{mz}, \tilde{P}_{mw})$
Normal	Model	$\mathbf{N} = (N_x, N_y, N_z)$
Texture coordinates	-	(u, v, q)
Pixel position fractions	-	f_{yl}, f_{yr}, f_x
Other data	Coordinate System	
Pixel coordinates	Post-perspective	$\mathbf{P} = (P_x, P_y, P_z, 1)$
Maximum displaced pixel coordinates	Post-perspective	$\mathbf{P}_\mathbf{m} = (P_{mx}, P_{my}, P_{mz}, 1)$
Perspective corrected texture coordinates	-	$(u', v') = (u/q, v/q)$
Displaced pixel coordinates	Perspective eye	$\check{\mathbf{D}} = (\tilde{D}_x, \tilde{D}_y, \tilde{D}_z, \tilde{D}_w)$
Perspective corrected displaced pixel coordinates	3D screen	$\mathbf{D} = (\tilde{D}_x/\tilde{D}_w, \tilde{D}_y/\tilde{D}_w, \tilde{D}_z/\tilde{D}_w)$

Table 3.2: Algorithm notation and rasterisation pipeline variables.

Another important consideration is the holes that will appear in the displaced surface if only the displaced pixels are rendered. In order to ensure a continuous surface without these holes or cracks, a new surface tesselated with triangles is generated with each triangle defined by three displaced surface points.

Figure 3.2 shows four adjacent pixels on two scan lines and their displaced positions on the new surface. In Figure 3.2 the pixels between the displaced pixels also need to be rendered. In this algorithm we propose to introduce two new triangles at each pixel displaced from the original surface. The two new triangles are shown shaded in Figure 3.2 and inside these triangles are pixels that would otherwise have been left vacant.

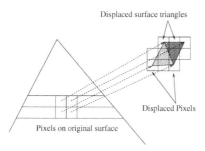

Figure 3.2: The two new triangles introduced at each pixel to cover pixels not rendered.

Therefore, displacement mapping is performed using a two pass rendering process, first remeshing, then final rendering. During the first stage, polygons describing the original surface are scan converted on a grid, with a coarser resolution than final screen space, resulting in sample points similiar to pixels on the original surface. In the second pass triangles defined by the displaced pixels (sample points) are rasterised into shaded screen pixels.

The notation used for coordinate values is the same as that used for the raster pipeline in Table 3.2. This notation will be used to indicate what values are stored at vertices and interpolated across scan lines.

3.1.1 Scan Conversion Algorithm Overview

The first phase of the scan conversion is based on the 'rational linear' rendering algorithm as presented by Heckbert and Moreton[35], also published in another form by Blinn[5]. This algorithm correctly interpolates texture coordinates and shading parameters for polygons viewed in perspective.

Before processing a triangle its orientation relative to the viewing direction is determined by taking the dot product between the viewing direction and the triangle's mean normal vector, transformed to world space. If the polygon is back facing it would normally be ignored and not rendered. For displacement mapping back facing polygons that are situated at the edge of an object can sometimes be displaced so as to make them become visible. It is impossible to determine which back facing triangles will become visible after displacement therefore all back facing triangles are rendered.

The algorithm is broken down into the following steps:

1. Limit minimum Y fraction stepping.

2. Round and displace vertices.

3. Setup triangle vertices and transform.

4. At each pixel :

    (a) Scan convert in coarse screen space.

    (b) Insert pixel remesh points along edges and snap remesh points to edges.

    (c) Displace surface.

    (d) Generate new triangles.

    (e) Render new triangles.

These steps will be expanded in the following sub-sections.

Limit Minimum Y Fraction Stepping

Indexing the displacement map using the (u, v) coordinates at particular points results in similar aliasing problems that are encountered with texture mapping. While a variety of solutions are available to the problem of texture mapping aliasing[34], they all use some form of averaging filter. Any filter applied to a displacement map with a high variance will return a single value for the height which may lose some of the detail present in the displacement map. Sampling problems when reading values from a displacement map will cause visible geometry popping artifacts. To minimise the effect of these artifacts we limit the minimum sampling rate to match the detail in the displacement map.

If the normal to a triangle is virtually perpendicular to the viewing direction then the triangle will be represented by only a few pixels in 3D screen space. Before sending a triangle to the primary scan conversion pipeline, we determine the orientation of the triangle, as explained earlier. To avoid aliasing problems we limit the minimum number of steps along the edges of the triangles and control the scan conversion process using the y fractions f_{yl} and f_{yr}[1] by setting an initial value and an incremental value[2]. The minimum number of steps along the triangle edges can be set based on the complexity of the displacement map provided by the user. Automatic calculation of the level of detail can be determined from the distance from the viewpoint, but ultimately it is the complexity of the displacement map that determines the necessary sampling. For the simple displacement maps and triangle sizes used for the examples in this chapter the minimum number of steps was set to 16.

Round and Displace Vertices

Once the vertices are projected into 3D screen space they are rounded to the nearest integer value. These rounded values are then transformed back into the model space and replace the original vertex values that are used for displacement and bilinear interpolation. To calculate the new displaced coordinates at each pixel the vertices of the triangle are displaced by the maximum displacement along the normals. This displacement is done in model space with the maximum displacement set to 1. This displacement of vertices to the maximally displaced position is shown in Figure 3.1 by the dotted lines at each vertex. If the triangle does not have different normals at each vertex then displacement only occurs at one vertex. Calculating the new coordinates of the displaced vertex at every vertex (using the normal at the vertex shared by neighbouring triangles) ensures that when a triangle mesh is rendered and the displacement map creates displacements along the edges of triangles there are no cracks between triangles in the triangle mesh.

---

[1]The fractional values for bilinear interpolation are described in Section 3.1.4

[2]A non-linear stepping function could be used to approximate perspective distortion in the Z direction.

Setup Triangle Vertices and Transform

At each triangle vertex V a record containing n parameters of interest is created $(r_1, r_2, \ldots, r_n)$ including texture coordinates. The original vertex coordinates E_x, E_y and E_z in world space are then transformed into perspective eye space. Any point P in this space will have a homogeneous coordinate $\tilde{P}_w$, different from zero, and we denote such points with a tilde. The transformed vertex becomes $\tilde{V} = (\tilde{V}_x, \tilde{V}_y, \tilde{V}_z, \tilde{V}_w)$. At each vertex, we also store the vertex coordinates in post-perspective space or non-homogeneous pixel coordinates, with the $\tilde{V}_w$ coordinate divided out. In post-perspective space, we omit the tilde to denote points: $V = (\tilde{V}_x/\tilde{V}_w, \tilde{V}_y/\tilde{V}_w, \tilde{V}_z/\tilde{V}_w, 1)$.

Parameters r_i and the number 1 are divided by $\tilde{V}_w$ to construct the variable list $(x, y, z, s_1, s_2, \ldots, s_{n+1})$, where $s_i = r_i/\tilde{V}_w$ for $i \leq n$, $s_{n+1} = 1/\tilde{V}_w$.

Scan Convert in Coarse Screen Space

The triangle is then scan converted in 3D screen space, with a resolution coarser than that of the final screen, and all parameters in the variable list $(s_1, s_2, \ldots, s_{n+1})$ are interpolated for each scan converted pixel and divided by s_{n+1} for each of the n parameters to yield perspective correct parameters. To ensure that the mesh of triangles is drawn without drawing any pixel twice and without leaving any holes, a scan conversion algorithm using half-open intervals is used[27].

Insert Pixel Remesh Points Along Edges and Snap Remesh Points to Edges

To ensure continuity across the displaced surface between triangle edges, remesh points are inserted along the edges of triangles. The pixel points, used as remeshing points calculated within each triangle, are moved or *snapped* to the edges of the triangle before displacement and retriangulation. If the gradient, m, of the edge satisfies $-1 <= m <= 1$ then remesh points are inserted along the edge with an x increment of 1, otherwise the points are inserted along the edge with a y increment of 1. To reduce the number of triangles generated and reduce the number of very small triangles these new edge remesh points are snapped to instead of used as new remesh points. In Figure 3.3 the new edge remesh points are shown in red, the original remesh points are shown as green filled squares if they are snapped to the new red remesh points on the triangle edges and unsnapped remesh points are left as black squares.

As each span of the triangle is processed remesh points at the beginning or end of a scan line next to an edge with new points inserted with y increments are

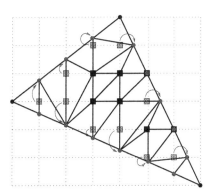

Figure 3.3: Remeshing points are snapped to the new edge remesh points which ensure matching sampling points along triangle edges.

snapped to the edge points by shifting them along the y axis. This case occurs for the right edge in Figure 3.3. When the new edge points are inserted with x increments then the original remesh points are snapped in the y direction to the edge remesh points. This is shown for the two left edges in Figure 3.3. When the current scan line is under the edge the remesh points are snapped up (top left edge in Figure 3.3) and when the edge is beneath the current scan line the remesh points are snapped down (bottom left edge in Figure 3.3). Since the new points inserted along the edge are dependent only on each edge's gradient, two neighbouring triangles will always have matching vertices inserted along their edges ensuring no T-vertices are produced.

Displace Surface

The interpolated (u, v, q) texture coordinate is divided by q and passed to a texture mapping engine to retrieve a displacement value from a displacement map in texture memory. To displace the current pixel S, $\tilde{P}$ and $\tilde{P}_m$ are linearly interpolated in eye space using the displacement ratio d:

$$\tilde{D} = d\tilde{P} + (1 - d)\tilde{P}_m \tag{3.1}$$

where d is the current displacement divided by the maximum displacement. The new displaced coordinate value $\tilde{D}$ is then divided by $\tilde{D}_w$ to generate the displaced pixel value D in 3D screen space.

Generate New Triangles

Using the displaced pixel and the coordinates of pixels from the previous scan line, one or two triangles are generated and then passed through a second rasterisation pipeline. Each pixel in the previous scan line of the current primitive must be kept for use by the triangle setup stage of the second pipeline. Also, already processed pixels in the current scan line must be kept. Using the pixels from the previous row and the previous pixel on the current scan line two new triangles can be formed from vertices $P(x,y), P(x,y-1), P(x-1,y-1)$ and $P(x,y), P(x-1,y-1), P(x-1,y)$. Both triangles belong to the displaced surface and are sent to a second pipeline for scan conversion.

Render New Triangles

New triangle vertices are sent to a second scan converter for final rendering, which could also be done by packing them as triangle strips.

3.1.2   Recomputing Normal Vectors

Recomputing the normals for the triangles of the displaced surface from geometry data would produce visible errors and is not well suited for hardware implementation. Depending on the pixel area subtended by the triangle, using the same normal for shading scan converted triangle pixels will show discontinuities between adjacent triangles. In order to maintain surface continuity and consistent shading, we derive new triangle normal vectors from a bump map to shade the displaced surface. For each scan converted pixel, normal vectors are recomputed by transforming the bump vectors read from the bump map to the rendered triangle by using the method described in Section 2.1.1 from[79].

Triangle normals could be calculated from the geometry of the newly constructed triangles. This would save on the transformation calculation of the bump vector using the first method. Unfortunately, this method does not account for shading continuity and produces poor results. A better normal approximation is obtained by reading a bump vector loaded from an analytically precomputed bump map and carrying out the transformation as explained above.

3.1.3 Generating Bump Maps from Height Fields

A displacement map can also be considered as a height field. The height field is defined by $F(u,v) = (u,v,h(u,v))$, where h denotes the bump height at (u,v). The normal vector N_P at a point P is expressed with:

$$N_P = \frac{\partial F}{\partial u} \times \frac{\partial F}{\partial v} = \begin{bmatrix} 1 \\ 0 \\ \frac{\partial h}{\partial u} \end{bmatrix} \times \begin{bmatrix} 0 \\ 1 \\ \frac{\partial h}{\partial v} \end{bmatrix} = \begin{bmatrix} -\frac{\partial h}{\partial u} \\ -\frac{\partial h}{\partial v} \\ 1 \end{bmatrix} \tag{3.2}$$

In order to support both displacement and bump mapping, we represent F by a grey scale image, where the set of discrete values is given by the pixel intensity. The grey scale intensity $F(u,v)$ corresponds to the amount by which a point of the surface shall be displaced.

By convolving the grey scale image representing the displacement map's height field with a two-dimensional central-differences filter kernel C respectively oriented with the u and v directions, we obtain an acceptable estimate of the two partial derivatives $\frac{\partial h}{\partial u}, \frac{\partial h}{\partial v}$.

$$\frac{\partial h}{\partial u} \approx C_u(P) \tag{3.3}$$

$$\frac{\partial h}{\partial v} \approx C_v(P) \tag{3.4}$$

$$C_u = \begin{bmatrix} -1 & 0 & 1 \\ -1 & 0 & 1 \\ -1 & 0 & 1 \end{bmatrix} \tag{3.5}$$

$$C_v = \begin{bmatrix} 1 & 1 & 1 \\ 0 & 0 & 0 \\ -1 & -1 & -1 \end{bmatrix} \tag{3.6}$$

The partial derivatives $\frac{\partial h}{\partial u}, \frac{\partial h}{\partial v}$ give the slope of the height field or bump function in the u and v directions and are proportional to the grey scale intensity transition in the u and v directions in the grey scale image.

Let us mention that deriving the bump vector by taking the cross product $\frac{\partial F}{\partial u} \times \frac{\partial F}{\partial v}$ works only if the parameterised target surface has orthogonal uv-lines, to which we can attach a local orthonormal coordinate system defined by e_u, e_v, e_w. For surfaces with non-orthogonal uv-lines, it is possible to build a local orthonormal system[79].

The chosen representation is sufficient in many cases, but does cause some aliasing artifacts if the grey scale resolution of the height field is too low to provide a smooth bump map, when sampled by the central-differences filter. For the example of the half-sphere bump pattern used in this chapter, this representation requires a higher grey scale resolution to properly sample the transitions between height values. Figure 3.4 compares the result obtained with a bump map generated from a grey scale image and a bump map that was computed analytically.

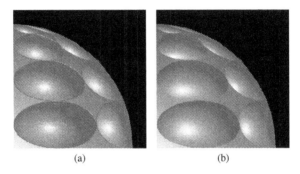

(a)   (b)

Figure 3.4: A close up of (a) a grey scale and (b) an analytically computed bump map.

3.1.4   Bilinear Interpolation of Vertex Coordinates

To ensure correct displacement mapping, displacement must occur in a linear space that is equivalent to the original model space. By bilinearly interpolating between maximum displaced vertices V_m using the fractional position of the current pixel in screen space it is possible to calculate coordinates in the appropriate coordinate system.

Figure 3.5 shows a triangle being scanned and the distances between the current pixel and the vertices that are used to calculate the bilinear interpolation. The fractional values are calculated using the following equations and the distances from Figure 3.5:

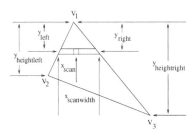

Figure 3.5: The calculation of the fractional values at the pixel.

$$f_{yl} = \frac{y_{left}}{y_{heightleft}} \tag{3.7}$$

$$f_{yr} = \frac{y_{right}}{y_{heightright}} \tag{3.8}$$

$$f_x = \frac{x_{scan}}{x_{scanwidth}} \tag{3.9}$$

The bilinear interpolation is :

$$U_r = U_1 + (U_3 - U_1)f_{yr} \tag{3.10}$$

$$U_l = U_1 + (U_2 - U_1)f_{yl} \tag{3.11}$$

$$T = U_l + (U_r - U_l)f_x \tag{3.12}$$

Using the bilinear equation and substituting the value of $\vec{V}_m$ at each vertex of the triangle for the corresponding U_k ($k = 1, 2, 3$), the value $\vec{P}_m$ is calculated from the result, T.

3.2 Hardware Architecture

Adding displacement mapping support to the standard rendering pipeline opens up different design alternatives. We will derive our architecture from the standard rasterisation pipelined architecture, in which scan converted pixels go through a texture and bump mapping stage. The proposed architectures couple two polygon rendering pipelines together for the proposed displacement mapping algorithm. The architecture for the displacement mapping algorithm is described in the next section followed by a a cheaper alternative architecture, a fully functioning dual pipeline approach and finally a discussion of performance issues.

3.2.1　Displacement Mapping Architecture

The displacement mapping engine uses scan conversion to calculate the screen pixel, P, and it's corresponding positional fractional values which are then used to bilinearly interpolate[3] the maximally displaced pixel, $\tilde{P}_m$, in eye space. The current pixel position, P is converted back to eye space, $\tilde{P}$. The new displaced value, $\tilde{D}$ is then calculated by linear interpolation between these two values in eye space and then transformed back to screen space, D.

To achieve this surface displacement either extra hardware has to be added to a single raster pipeline that performs buffering to allow both passes or an extra raster pipeline is added at the front of a standard raster pipeline. In the dual pipeline case the first raster pipeline effectively generates new triangles on the displaced surface and sends them to the second triangle rendering pipeline. Alternatively, looping back into the same rendering pipeline would mean that triangles generated by the first pass would stall the processing of the original mesh while the second pass is performed and result in lower performance in terms of rendered polygons per frame. Though the insertion of FIFOs and memory to buffer temporary data would reduce the effect of pipeline stalls on performance, the use of only one pipeline for both passes does provide automatic load balancing instead of in the dual pipeline case where either pipeline could be idle while waiting for the other pipeline to be ready.

In the two pipeline case both the primary and secondary pipeline contain all the stages for triangle scan conversion (triangle setup, edge walk, span generation). The first pipeline requires a texture mapping engine to retrieve the displacement value from the displacement map stored in memory. The per-pixel operations such as texture and bump mapping are also necessary for the second pass, since pixels belonging to the displacement mapped surface get textured or bump mapped only during the second pass.

The basic computational units for an architecture using two pipelines is shown in Figure 3.6. The basic units shown in Figure 3.6 are based on the triangle raster

---

[3]See Section 3.1.4.

pipeline as described by Kugler[49]. The variables processed by each stage are listed in Table 3.2.

To render triangles a scan conversion algorithm based on half-open intervals[27] is used which ensures there are no holes or overlaps between adjacent triangles. The initial triangle setup is responsible for setting up the triangle and expects all transformations of vertices to be done by the host or a separate geometry transformation pipeline. The edge walk phase decomposes triangles into horizontal spans and spans into pixels. The edge walk moves along the edges of the triangle generating the starting and ending x values for a span. It is also reponsible for generating the fractional values f_{yl} and f_{yr}. These fractional values are the fraction the current step is along the respective edges from the top vertex to the bottom vertex. The span generation calculates the values at each pixel and also the fractional value f_x. To process the spans an iterator is used for each of the variables shown in Table 3.2. The span generator generates one pixel per cycle in the x-direction.

The Bilinear Interpolation unit performs it's calculations in eye space requiring the fractional values f_{yl}, f_{yr} and f_x to be converted back into eye space by dividing them with the interpolated q coordinate because the fractional pixel positions are calculated incrementally in screen space during scan conversion.

Section 3.1.4 describes the calculation required for the Bilinear Interpolation unit. The Bilinear Interpolation unit has 6 multiply units with latencies of approximately 5 each. The total latency of the Bilinear Interpolation unit is 6 including the subtraction and addition. This latency is easily accommodated by the latency of the perspective divide pipeline. The major cost for perspective correct displacement mapping is the extra area required for the 6 multipliers.

The Displaced Surface Generator stores the previous and current scan-line pixel data and uses this to generate new triangles or send the pixel data to the per-pixel operations in the second raster pipeline. The per-pixel operations in the second pipeline include a texture mapping engine, Phong shading, colour and z-buffer interfaces. Since the new triangles are generated by the second stage the normal N is interpolated as shown in the first span generator. For triangles being sent to the second raster pipeline the normal will be further interpolated before being Phong shaded in the per-pixel operations. The stage carrying out Phong shading either has to transform the interpolated normal vector to world space or make the lighting computation in model space, since normal vector interpolation and bump mapping happens in model space. Accurate perspective division at pixel rates can be costly so approximation techniques would be employed[28, 88, 26]. The per-pixel operations also include writing pixel data to the colour and z-buffer.

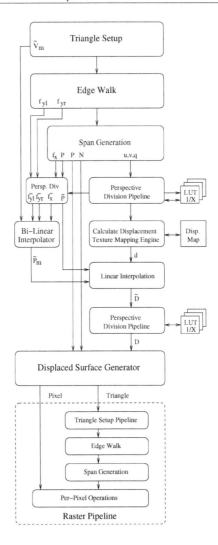

Figure 3.6: Displacement mapping pipeline using bilinear interpolation and a dual pipeline.

3.2.2   A Cheaper Architecture

The previous architecture carries out displacement mapping in eye space, before
carrying out the perspective division to go from eye space to 3D screen space. A
more cost effective alternaive is to process parameters $P_m = (P_{mx}, P_{my}, P_{mz}, 1)$ and
$P = (P_x, P_y, P_z, 1)$ in a similar way to the interpolation of texture coordinates. Instead of being iterpolated in eye space, maximum displaced triangle pixels are interpolated in the same way as texture coordinates and transformed back by another
perspective divide, before making the displacement of the current pixel. Interpolating P and P_m would be followed by an extra division to bring both parameters
back to eye space: parameters $(P_{mx}, P_{my}, P_{mz}, 1)$ and $(P_x, P_y, P_z, 1)$ are divided by q.
In the previous approach, parametes $\tilde{P}$ and $\tilde{P}_m$ do not require perspective division
after interpolation, but can be used as such to linearly interpolate the displaced
vertex $\tilde{D}$.

The changes to the previous architecture are shown in Figure 3.7. The second
stage of the piepline is not shown since it is unchanged from the first architecture.
The difference to the previous approach is how base triangles and triangles subtended by maximum displaced vertices get sampled. In this architecture, these are
sampled in screen space and pixels are transformed back to a linear space. The
major advantage is the removal of the complexity of the Bilinear Interpolation
Unit, but the cost is poor performance for some triangles.

The problem with this approach is that the pixel on the displaced triangle,
P_m, is scanned converted along with the base triangle and this will only work if
the two triangles are the same shape in screen space. If the normals of the base
triangle are very different then the resulting maximally displaced triangle will be
scan converted incorrectly and produce poor results.

This architecture could be further improved by performing the linear interpolation in screen space using the following formula :

$$D = \frac{d}{q}P + (1 - \frac{d}{q})P_m \qquad (3.13)$$

This reduces the number of perspective divisions from three down to one.
This will only produce errors for triangles that are large and very close to the view
plane.

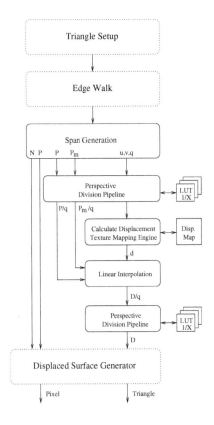

Figure 3.7: A cheaper displacement mapping triangle raster pipeline.

3.2.3   Dual Pipelines with a Displacement Mapping Unit

Another alternative is to have two identical rendering pipelines, both containing a texture and bump mapping stage, but sharing a displacement mapping unit. When both pipelines run in displacement mapping mode, one of the pipelines scan converts polygons of the original surface using the displacement mapping unit and passes the triangles of the displaced surface to the other pipeline for texture mapping and shading. Standard rendering of polygons with no displacement mapping can be carried out by both pipelines running in parallel to achieve a higher throughput. Additionally, the dual pipelines can provide multi-texturing support to create special effects like blending or transparency effects.

3.2.4   Performance

Several factors affect the performance of the displacement mapping architecture. The overall triangle throughput performance is determined by the remeshing resolution of the first pass. The closer the resolution of the first pass to the final screen resolution the greater the number of triangles generated by this first pass and hence the lower the performance. The added displacement mapping steps in the first pipeline have a roughly equivalent latency to the per-pixel processing steps removed. This results in the latency of the dual pipeline displacement mapping architecture to be effectively double that of a standard raster pipeline.

3.3   Results

To test the described algorithm a software simulation was written and a sphere made up of 1280 triangles was rendered with texture, bump and displacement mapping and the results are shown in Figure 3.8 and Figure 3.9. In Figure 3.8(b) and Figure 3.9(b) a bumpy silhouette is now noticeable. The bumps in the middle of the spheres show very little difference except in the position of the highlight which has moved due to the new position of the specular highlight on the displaced surface. In Figure 3.8(b) and Figure 3.9(b) the effect of back facing polygons can also be noticed by the new row of bumps on the very outside of the sphere.

Figure 3.10 shows a few examples of the kind of surface displacement possible with only two simple displacement maps and surface colour textures[4] Of the six images four are made using only a simple half sphere displacement map and

---

[4]The texture images are from the 3DCAFE web site.

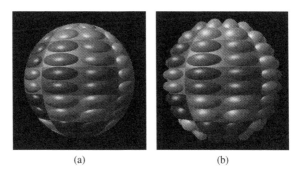

(a)   (b)

Figure 3.8: A sphere with (a) bump mapping only and (b) bump mapping and displacement mapping.

the other two with a half torus displacement map. These figures show complex surfaces generated from a few simple primitives that would require much greater geometry bandwidth to the graphics card and transformation calculation without displacement mapping.

3.4 Summary

This chapter presented a new method of displacement mapping that can be implemented into standard 3D graphics hardware. By using typical scan conversion plus one extra parameter and three extra vertex transformations, the surface can be displaced at every pixel, retriangulated and rendered using a standard raster graphics pipeline. This displacement mapping method offers the ability to render displaced surfaces at real time rates using a triangle mesh and a displacement map.

This algorithm could be extended to work with alternative polygon rendering algorithms such as stamp based rasterisation[60].

The next chapter, Chapter 4, presents a hardware architecture for displacement mapping that generates triangles that more accurately represent the underlying surface represented by the displacement map by adaptively sampling the displacement map. The technique in the next chapter requires calculations to be performed in both object and screen space. This assumes the availability of a

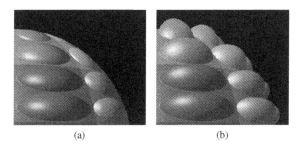

(a)   (b)

Figure 3.9: A close up of the sphere with (a) bump mapping only and (b) bump mapping and displacement mapping.

viewing transformation unit (geometry engine) in hardware. Furthermore several data transfers must be made past this geometry engine. In comparison the architecture presented in this chapter only requires a rasterisation unit to be available in hardware.

Figure 3.10: Several examples of a displacement mapped sphere using only two displacements maps but with varying parameters.

Chapter 4

Adaptive Displacement Mapping using Tessellation

This chapter presents a new approach to displacement mapping based on recursive tessellation that adapts to the surface complexity described by the displacement map. It also ensures that the resolution of the displaced mesh is tessellated with respect to the current view point. The tessellation scheme performs all tests only on triangle edges to avoid generating cracks on the displaced surface. The main decision for vertex insertion is based on two comparisons involving the average height surrounding the vertices and the normals at the vertices. Individually, the tests will fail to tessellate a mesh satisfactorily, but their combination achieves good results. The implementation of this architecture involves the introduction of several additions to the typical hardware rendering pipeline in order to achieve displacement map rendering in hardware. The mesh tessellation is placed within the rendering pipeline in order to take advantage of the pre-existing vertex transformation units to perform the setup calculations for the view dependent test. This method adds only simple arithmetic and comparison operations to the graphics pipeline and makes use of existing units for calculations wherever possible.

To apply a displacement map to a triangle mesh involves re-triangulating the original mesh and displacing the vertices accordingly. If the base triangle mesh has a coarser resolution than the displacement map we need to re-tessellate the mesh according to the surface defined by the displacement map. This re-tessellation can be performed while rasterizing the triangle as presented in Gumhold[32] and the previous chapter. The problem with these approaches is that either a large number of triangles is generated or new coordinate systems and complex calculations in a non-standard rasterizer are required to control the pipeline[32].

The algorithm presented in this chapter tessellates each triangle individually by recursively adding vertices along edges in order to achieve an adaptively tessellated surface. Local surface variation is checked between vertices by comparing normals. At the same time the average displacement over an area around the vertices is checked—to avoid the aliasing caused by sampling—using Summed-Area Tables as presented by Crow[11]. These two tests applied individually do not generate good results, since the normal test results in aliasing and the averaged height test misses small details, but the combination of the two tests produces good results. To give the user control over the size of triangles generated with respect to the current view point, the screen size of triangles is tested against a user threshold. This ensures that recursive tessellation will stop when the user does not require further detail. A displacement map models a discrete surface which has a limit of resolution. We also check if this limit is reached before generating more triangles, to ensure no more triangles are generated then there is detail in the original displacement map.

To minimise the additional hardware required to render displacement maps, we exploit existing pipeline units wherever possible. A bump mapping unit is used for displaced surface normal calculation and extra units are carefully placed within the pipeline to make use of the operations performed by the transformation unit. The remaining computations only require simple operations such as addition, division by two and comparisons.

4.1   Adaptive View Dependent Tessellation

Our algorithm recursively tessellates the triangles given in the base mesh or surface $\mathbf{P}(u, v)$ by inserting vertices along edges of triangles. A base triangle that has been recursively adaptively tessellated to increase the number of vertices in the area of height change is shown in Figure 4.1.

4.1.1   Tessellation based only on edge information

Displacement mapping requires a coarse triangle mesh that approximates the surface to be modelled with a displacement map containing the finer geometric detail. A re-meshing step is required to generate a finer mesh that better represents the desired surface. While many re-meshing algorithms exist[30], few are suitable for hardware implementation. For example, if tessellation decisions are based on information local to one triangle then the neighbouring triangles would need ac-

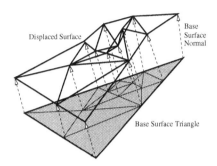

Figure 4.1: A triangle from the base surface is recursively tessellated to create a displaced surface.

cess to this information requiring processing of each triangle to have access to the entire triangle list. Random access to memory of this nature is expensive when implemented in hardware. To avoid such memory requirements, we limit our vertex insertion decision to using only the information available within the current triangle. Furthermore if vertex insertion decisions use all three vertices of a triangle then the common edge between two adjacent triangles may have a different insertion decision due to the third triangle vertex. Vertices inserted along the edge of one triangle but not inserted on the same edge of a neighbouring triangle are known as t-vertices. To avoid cracking in the displaced surface t-vertices must be avoided. To ensure no t-vertices are generated we limit our vertex insertion decision to information contained in only the two vertices that subtend the edge in question. The tradeoff is that calculations for each edge are performed twice.

Re-meshing is performed by inserting vertices at the midpoint of edges if the midpoint meets a series of conditions. First the new vertex $\mathbf{P}_{12}$ between the two vertices $\mathbf{P}_1, \mathbf{P}_2$ of an edge is calculated by averaging the two vertices. The texture coordinates $\mathbf{U}_{12}$ and the mesh normal $\mathbf{N}_{12}$ are similarly calculated. The normal on the displaced surface, $\mathbf{N}'$ can be calculated from the original mesh normal, $\mathbf{N}$ and the normal calculated from the displacement map, $\mathbf{N}_D$, using the bump mapping operations described by Schilling [79]. The normal to the displacement map, $D(u, v)$ can be precomputed using finite differencing and stored in a normal map in a similar fashion to RGB values stored in texture maps. The displaced surfaces and normals are shown in Figure 2.1.

4.1.2 Surface Normal Variance Test

Using the new surface normal, $\mathbf{N}'_{12}$, we compare it's components with those of the two displaced vertex normals, $\mathbf{N}'_1$ and $\mathbf{N}'_2$. If the difference between any of the components is greater than a set threshold, then a vertex is added at $\mathbf{P}_{12}$ (*Normal Test*). The boolean value for the Normal Test, nt is defined as

$$
\begin{aligned}
nt \;=\; & (\mathbf{N}'_{12x} - \mathbf{N}'_{1x} < nthr)|(\mathbf{N}'_{12y} - \mathbf{N}'_{1y} < nthr)| \\
& (\mathbf{N}'_{12z} - \mathbf{N}'_{1z} < nthr)|(\mathbf{N}'_{12x} - \mathbf{N}'_{2x} < nthr)| \\
& (\mathbf{N}'_{12y} - \mathbf{N}'_{2y} < nthr)|(\mathbf{N}'_{12z} - \mathbf{N}'_{2z} < nthr)
\end{aligned}
\tag{4.1}
$$

where $nthr$ is the normal threshold and the | symbol represents the logical *or* operation.

The Normal Test is subject to aliasing because it uses point sampling and can easily miss changes in height. A simple example of this is shown in Figure 4.3(a). The advantage of the Normal Test is that it is extremely sensitive to small scale changes in the surface. The user is required to predetermine the threshold value $nthr$ and supply this value with the mesh to achieve the required level of detail.

4.1.3 Local Area Average Height Test

To detect average changes in the height of the displacement map, a second test is performed that compares the displacement over an area using Summed-Area Tables, introduced by Crow [11]. A Summed-Area Table is a two dimensional array containing at each cell the sum of all values that fall inside the rectangle formed by that cell and one corner of the array. To calculate the sum of all values within a rectangular area in the table only the four values at the corners of the area are needed. The Summed-Area Table can be represented as a bivariate function $SAT(x,y)$ that returns the sum of all heights within the region $(0 \rightarrow x, 0 \rightarrow y)$, where the origin is in the bottom left of the table. The sum of the values within a rectangular area are calculated using the function $S(\mathbf{Z})$ defined as

$$
\begin{aligned}
S(\mathbf{Z}) \;=\; & SAT(x_{tr}, y_{tr}) - SAT(x_{tl}, y_{tl}) - \\
& SAT(x_{br}, y_{br}) + SAT(x_{bl}, y_{bl})
\end{aligned}
\tag{4.2}
$$

where $\mathbf{Z}$ is $(x_{tr}, y_{tr}, x_{tl}, y_{tl}, x_{br}, y_{br}, x_{bl}, y_{bl})$, the corners of the rectangular area in the Summed-Area Table, using the subscripts tr top right, tl top left, br bottom right, bl bottom left for the four corners of the rectangle .

A Summed-Area Table can be precalculated for the displacement map and the sum of all heights over an area at vertices P_1, P_2 and P_{12} can be calculated. To calculate the four corner points of the rectangle around the vertices of the edge we use the texture coordinates at the vertices U_1, U_2 and U_{12} as shown in Figure 4.2. Using the texture coordinates we can calculate the difference of the areas and

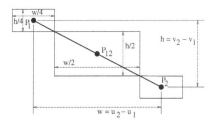

Figure 4.2: Using the texture coordinates of the vertices to calculate the summed height.

compare them with a threshold. This test is called the *Summed Height Test* and its boolean value, *sht*, is defined as

$$sht = \left(\frac{S(P_{12})}{2} - (S(P_1) + S(P_2)) \right) < shthr \qquad (4.3)$$

where *shthr* is the summed height threshold. This test misses some cases that the Normal Test detects as shown in Figure 4.3(b). In Figure 4.3 the solid line represents a contour line across the displacement map between the texture coordinates of the vertices of one edge of a triangle with the newly inserted point in the middle. The dashed lines indicate the area over which the height is averaged to calculate the Summed Height value. In Figure 4.3(a) the Normal Test fails, but the Summed Height Test succeeds. In Figure 4.3(b) the Normal Test succeeds but the Summed Height Test fails. There are cases that cannot be detected by both tests. If the displacement map is highly regular, e.g. high frequency such as a sinusoidal function, then the Normal Test could always sample identical normals and the height averaging would cancel itself out. Typically a displacement map and associated triangle mesh are created together by the author with the purpose of modelling a particular surface so these cases can be avoided. The combination of the Normal Test and Summed Height Test with appropriate thresholds is capable of re-meshing the small detail in a surface without missing height changes in smooth surfaces resulting in effective filtering of the displacement map.

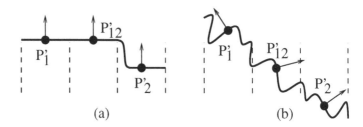

(a)   (b)

Figure 4.3: Tessellation edge tests. In (a) only the Summed Height Test succeeds. In (b) only the Normal Test succeeds.

Displacement Map Filtering

The standard approach for texture filtering is mipmapping as presented by Williams[89]. This provides an effective means of retrieving levels of detail in colour textures that match the screen size of an object. But for displacement mapping, the averaging effect of mipmapping will smooth over areas of detail in the displacement map. In [32], they propose to use mipmapping, but with a maximal filter to overcome this. The Summed Height Test can still miss details due to averaging over the height, but the normal test will find these details. And conversely, when the Normal test fails to detect height change over a smooth surface, the Summed Height Test will detect the change. This combination results in an effective filtering of the displacement map.

4.1.4   View Dependent Resampling

To achieve a view dependent re-sampling that ensures no new triangles are generated once a certain screen size has been reached, we perform a test based on the size of the current edge in Screen Space. This test can be performed after the vertices $\mathbf{P}'_1$ and $\mathbf{P}'_2$ of the current edge are transformed into Screen Space by

carefully placing the re-meshing hardware within an existing graphics pipeline. Calculating the Euclidean distance requires expensive square and square root operations, so we only use a Manhattan distance calculation between the two screen space vertices. This Manhattan distance is compared with a threshold measured in number of pixels. This test is called the *View Test* and if the Manhattan distance is greater then a threshold measured in number of pixels, $vthr$ then the boolean value vt is set to true.

4.1.5 Refinement Limit Test

Height fields can be rendered by first generating a mesh by inserting the points defined by the height field into a mesh using algorithms such as the Greedy Insertion Algorithm[30]. These algorithms pass over the complete mesh and determine the point of maximum error and insert that point. In the algorithm presented here, we only insert points calculated from the vertices of triangle edges as they are easy to compute and only depend on the local information of a single edge. If we want to insert points inside a triangle, then the other vertex in a triangle is required to calculate the interpolated normal at the point inside the triangle. Another problem occrs when an adjacent triangle calculates that a point to be inserted is outside its triangle and is actually inside an adjacent triangle, then the triangle needs access to the vertex in the adjacent triangle.

The alternative of only inserting points on edges leads to the problem that the points defined by the displacement map are only approximated and several points might be inserted close to the original point due to this approximation error. To stop the recursive algorithm from over inserting points when the original resolution of the displacement map is reached, we perform a test on the texture coordinates of the new point. We compare the integer values of the texture coordinates after they are scaled to the resolution of the displacement map. If the value of both integer parts of the texture coordinates at the newly inserted vertex U_{12} are equal to either of the scaled values of the two original vertices U_1 and U_2, then the new vertex is not inserted and the boolean value, ct is set to false. The test is called the *Tex Coord Test*. This test stops recursive subdivision, once the resolution of the original displacement map is reached. We have found that models with areas of high variance of the displacement map, such as the hair on the model of Volker Blanz's head (see Figure 9), can reduce their final triangle counts by up to 50% by incorporating this simple test.

An alternative to performing the Tex Coord Test is to precalculate the points on the new surface $\mathbf{P}'(u, v)$ and store them with the displacement map. These

values can then be inserted instead of inserting midpoints resulting in a more accurate representation of the original displacement map. The problem with this technique is that the displacement map cannot be interactively scaled because the new surface has already been pre-calculated.

4.1.6   Tessellation

Once all the tests have been performed for an edge of a triangle the decision to split the edge is calculated using the following logic equation

$$split = (nt|sht)\&vt\&ct \qquad (4.4)$$

where | represents the logical *or* operation and & represents the logical *and* operation. This *split* value is calculated for each edge and depending on the number of edges that have to be split an appropriate tessellation is chosen from Figure 4.4(a-c). The tessellation shown in Figure 4.4(a) is used if three edges are to be split, Figure 4.4(b) is used if two edges are split and Figure 4.4(c) is used when one edge is split. Figure 4.4(d) shows two other possibilities for tessellating case 4.4(c), but we found that these two triangulations increased the occurance of long and thin triangles so we used the triangulation shown in (c) instead.

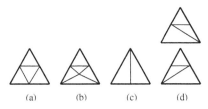

(a)   (b)   (c)   (d)

Figure 4.4: The three triangulations used for tessellation (a,b,c). (d) Two other possibilities for splitting two edges.

4.1.7   Curved Surface rendering using Displacement Maps

One problem for the rendering of displacement maps in hardware is that modellers are not used to thinking in terms of generating models from displacement maps.

In order to handle higher order primitives such as quadric curves, bezier surfaces and NURBS using our algorithm, we have incorporated into our displacement mapping software simulation the capability to sample a quadric surface and render it using displacement mapping. The current software implementation has only limited capabilities, since it can only render NURBS which only elevate their parameter space.

The only information that can be stored in the NURBS surface is the height or displacement from a base mesh. Applied to a suitable base mesh, this already provides enormous flexibility for designing and modelling by exploiting the high triangle performance of available graphics cards. Although this sampling approach uses the host to compute the displacement map, it would be relatively straightforward to couple a hardware implementation of a curved surface evaluation – like that used in the OpenGL pipeline proposed by Rockwood[77] – with our hardware design, if they become available in the future. This would enable the rendering of curved surface models at high speed and without the need for new and expensive scanline converters.

4.2   Hardware Architecture

To realise hardware rendering of displacement maps, we suggest the introduction of several units into a standard rendering pipeline such as the OpenGL pipeline[92]. These new units and their positioning relative to the usual units in a pipeline are shown in Figure 4.5. The OpenGL *Clipping, Perspective, and Viewport Application stage* is represented by our Transform stage. The OpenGL pipeline places Lighting inside the Vertices operations unit before transformation to screen space to achieve per-vertex lighting. Modern implementations of the graphics pipeline such as NVIDIA's GPUs place the lighting calculations after the transformation to improve per-fragment lighting capabilities. We have also moved the Lighting stage after the Transform stage, to allow our re-meshing and normal calculations to occur in world space.

We add four new units to the graphics pipeline including a *Get Triangle, Calculate New* **P**, *Displace Vertex, Tessellation Tests* and *Tessellation* stage. Also storage for the displacement map and a triangle queue are added at the top level. The Get Triangle Unit is responsible for retrieving triangles from either the host CPU or the Triangle Queue. The Get Triangle Unit also checks which vertices and normals of incoming triangles have already been transformed into screen space and only sends the new vertices and their normals through the Transform unit.

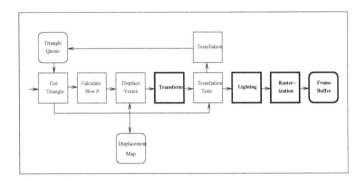

Figure 4.5: A graphics pipeline with new units added to perform displacement map rendering.

The Calculate New **P** stage takes two vertices of a triangle and averages them to find the midpoint. This midpoint passes through the Displace Vertex stage which calculates the new surface point $\mathbf{P}'(\mathbf{u}, \mathbf{v})$ as defined in Equation 2.6. This requires reading the displacement D from the displacement map, multiplying it by the surface normal $\hat{\mathbf{N}}$ and adding the result to the current surface point **P**. This operation is only performed for new vertices which are extracted from the current triangle information by the Get Triangle stage. Once the displacement is performed, the newly displaced vertex is passed through the Transform stage and transformed into screen space. The Tessellation stage takes the vertex information of the current triangle, the new vertices to be inserted, and constructs new triangles based on the triangulations shown in Section 4.1.6. These new triangles are inserted into the Triangle Queue, a FIFO queue, where they are read back into the pipeline by the Get Triangle unit. The Triangle Queue requires either on-chip memory or off-chip memory requiring an additional reading and writing unit. Either implementation is a significant requirement for this algorithm.

4.2.1   Tessellation Tests Architecture

The Tessellation Tests unit calculates new texture coordinates and normals and the four edge tests. The unit is pipelined and each new vertex, $\mathbf{P}_{12}, \mathbf{P}_{23}$ and $\mathbf{P}_{31}$, is sent through the pipeline sequentially, requiring only one pipeline. If faster performance was required due to multiple Transform pipelines then the unit could be replicated three times. The architecture of the Tessellation Tests unit is shown in Figure 4.6 with inputs and outputs labelled for testing the edge between vertices $\mathbf{P}_1$ and $\mathbf{P}_2$.

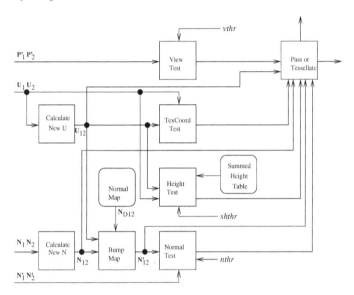

Figure 4.6: Architecture for the Tessellation Tests unit.

View Test

The simplest test in the Tessellation Tests is the View Test. This test is done in screen space by calculating the Manhattan distance for the current edge using the displaced transformed vertices. For triangles that are being re-tessellated, the transformed vertex values will have already been calculated in the previous pass, so this data will be immediately available. But for new triangles, this stage will have to wait until the values are available after the Transform stage. This waiting time can be easily accommodated, since for each new triangle the tests must wait until not only the original vertices are transformed, but also the newly inserted vertices are transformed. Also the ratio of new triangles to re-tessellated triangles is quite low so this wait time will happen infrequently. The result of the View Test, *vt* is passed to the Pass or Tessellate unit.

Tex Coord Test

The calculation of the texture coordinates for the new vertices is required by several subsequent units. The *Calculate New U* calculates the new texture coordinates using an add and division by two. The integer part of the new texture coordinate up to the resolution of the displacement map are compared with the integer part of the original texture coordinates of the edge's vertices. The test is calculated by the *Tex Coord Test* unit and the result passed onto the Pass or Tessellate unit.

Summed Height Test

The new texture coordinates are used by the *Height Test* to look up and calculate an average height from the *Summed Height Table*. First the difference between the texture coordinates at the vertices are calculated and divided by 4 and 8 using logical shift operations. The results are combined with the vertex texture coordinates to calculate the four values required to access the Summed Height Table. The calculation of the average height for each point using the Summed Height Table will take four cycles since each value must be read and combined using Equation 4.2. The values are then combined and divided according to the Summed Height Test and the difference compared with the *shthr* to determine if there is a significant change in height. The result is passed to the Pass or Tessellate unit.

Normal Test

The other operation of the Tessellation Tests unit is the Normal Test. This test requires first the calculation of the new normal $\mathbf{N}_{12}$ using an add and division by two. Then the new normal must be normalised before being bump mapped. Normalisation is an expensive operation, but implementations are available in most graphics pipelines. Then using the new texture coordinates, the normal to the displacement $\mathbf{N}_D$ is read from a precomputed normal map. The new surface normal,

N'_{12} is calculated by perturbing the surface normal, N_{12}, by the displacement map normal, N_D, using a bump mapping hardware unit. As mentioned earlier several approaches to bump mapping have been proposed and could be used to provide the operation required here. After calculating the new displaced surface normal its components are subtracted from those of the normals from the displaced vertices N'_1 and N'_2. The difference is compared to *nthr* resulting in the boolean value *nt* which is passed to the Pass or Tessellate unit.

Pass or Tessellate Unit

The Pass or Tessellate unit combines the results of the four tests to determine if the edge is to be split. If the edge is to be split then the new vertex P'_{12} is indicated for insertion into the current triangle to the Tessellation unit. For each vertex that was part of the original triangle, the Pass or Tessellate unit passes the following set of values to the Tessellation unit : $P_w, P'_s, N, N', N'_s, U$ where the subscript $_w$ means the vector is in world space and the subscript $_s$ means the vector is in screen space. For the newly inserted vertices, it has all of the above values except the N'_s value which is calculated on the triangles next pass through the pipeline. If the triangle has no new vertices to insert then only the following values are sent to the Lighting unit P'_s, N'_s, U. The Pass or Tessellate unit can also perform backface culling on the new triangles since they have been generated with screen space normal values.

The most complex unit in the Tessellation Tests unit are those required for the Normal Test which include a bump mapping operation and a normalisation. Both units exist in most graphics pipelines and can be expected in most pipelines in the future. Also memory and a controller for the buffering in the Triangle Queue is required. The other units only require addition, subtraction, divisions by powers of two, compare operations and other logic functions. The latency involved in the Tessellation Tests unit can be compensated by the latency of the Transform unit since both pipelines run in parallel. The major additional latency to the overall graphics pipeline is in the Displace Vertex unit which requires a multiply and accumulate.

4.3   Results

To demonstrate the effectiveness of our adaptive tessellation algorithm, we have implemented the architecture in Figure 4.5 and Figure 4.6 using a software simulation. To take advantage of OpenGL functionality, we use the feedback render mode to perform the transform calculations. We have rendered several models with our technique to demonstrate the range of datasets that it can handle and possibilities provided by displacement mapping.

To demonstrate the adaptive nature of the tessellation and the effectiveness of combining the Normal Test and Summed Height Test, a flat plane consisting of only 18 triangles was displaced with a half donut displacement as shown in Figure 4.7. In Figure 4.7(a), we can see the aliasing errors associated with the Normal Test, while in Figure 4.7(b), some edges have not been split because the averaging effect of the Summed Height Test has not detected the local change in surface orientation. The combination of the two tests is shown in Figure 4.7(c) where both the local surface orientation and average change in height is detected producing an adaptively tessellated displaced surface.

The view dependent capabilities of our algorithm are demonstrated using a cyberware scanner model of Volker Blanz's head. The scanner generates a texture and displacement map parametrised in cylindrical coordinates with a resolution of 512×456 texels. We use a cylinder for a base mesh consisting of 1800 triangles. The model rendered at three different distances from the view point is shown in Figure 4.8. In Figures 4.8(a), (b) and (c), the image rendered shows the distance of the model from the view plane. In Figures 4.8(d), (e) and (f), a wireframe close-up of the region around the nose, eyes and mouth using the respective meshes from (a), (b) and (c), can be seen. In Figure 4.8(d) the high level of detail can be seen in the tessellation around the eye including the eye brow. Both the view dependent tessellation as well as the effective adaptive techniques are demonstrated. The adaptive nature of the algorithm can be seen in the level of detail around the nose, eyes and mouth where there is increased surface detail.

To evaluate the algorithm on terrain models, we used the Crater Lake (West half of Crater Lake, Oregon) Digital Elevation Map (DEM), which has dimensions of 366×459 from Garland[30]. In Figure 4.9 we can see that a small island inside the crater and the edge of the crater is represented with a high level of detail, while the water level in the crater is left at the resolution of the original mesh.

An example of the donut displacement map applied to the well-known Utah teapot is shown in Figure 4.10(a). We are also investigating the possibilities of saving the mesh state from one displacement map and adding another displacement to it as shown in Figure 4.10(b) where the base donut is a displacement map. While this works in our software simulation we are still considering the hardware implications of such an operation.

(a)

(b)

(c)

Figure 4.7: (a) Normal Test only. (b) Summed Height Test only. (c) Both tests.

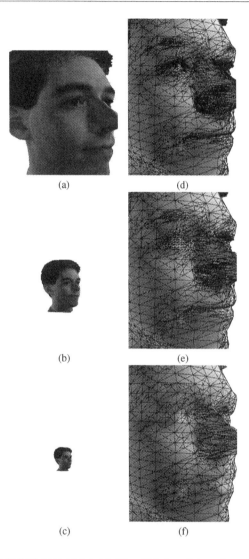

Figure 4.8: Volker's head dataset. (a), (b) and (c) show distance from view plane, (d), (e) and (f) are mesh close-ups for corresponding images.

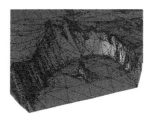

Figure 4.9: The Crater Lake

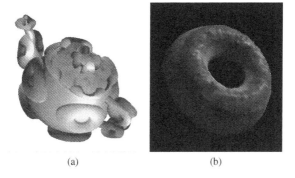

(a)   (b)

Figure 4.10: (a) A half donut displaced teapot (b) The half donut with texture and more surface detail added using another displacement map.

4.4   Summary

This chapter proposed several additional units for a standard graphics pipeline to enable the rendering of displacement maps in hardware. The technique encompasses adaptive view dependent re-meshing, driven by the displacement map's surface complexity and user defined thresholds. The additions to the hardware pipeline would only require standard features such as bump mapping and simple arithmetic units. The algorithm was tested on several real and synthetic datasets and it is capable of generating low triangle count meshes, by adaptively subdividing triangles. The tessellation scheme takes into account several factors including displacement, surface variation, view point and original mesh resolution. Backface culling cannot be applied to the original base mesh, because the displacement might generate triangles that are visible. The tessellation results in normals in screen space, so backface culling can be applied after tessellation and before rasterization. The combination of the Normal Test with the Summed Height Test also provides an effective filter for the displacement map, which is not possible using maximal valued mipmapping. Using displacement mapping as a rendering primitive can significantly reduce the bottleneck of sending triangle data to the graphics engine.

The cost of displacement mapping is an increase in pipeline size and latency which can be accommodated given ever increasing die sizes and higher clock frequencies. Displacement mapping brings new levels of visual realism to real time 3D graphics systems and could be incorporated into next generation graphics systems. As displacement maps are used increasingly to model the geometric detail on surfaces, hardware support for rendering these displacement maps will become a sought-after feature in graphics accelerators.

There are several avenues of future work that are possible from what has been presented in the last two chapters. Scaling the displacement map by introducing a scaling factor s into Equation 2.6 is done as follows

$$\mathbf{P}'(u,v) = \mathbf{P}(u,v) + sD(u,v)\hat{\mathbf{N}}(u,v) \tag{4.5}$$

The capability to scale the displacement map already exists within our software simulation, but requires that the displacement value used in the Displace Vertex unit is appropriately scaled and that the normal map is calculated using finite differences and is normalised for each new scale value of the displacement map. Another interesting extension to our work includes tests on the surface normals to determine which triangles are located within or near the Phong highlight to improve the tessellation of these area when per-vertex lighting schemes are used.

Also the automatic generation of the threshold levels from the displacement map would improve the simplicity of the algorithm.

The integration of Subdivision Surfaces with the adaptive scheme has been investigated by Amor, Boo et al.[2]. A highly memory efficient meshing scheme suitable for implementation as a hardware architecture was developed.

Part II

Volume Rendering

Chapter 5

An Efficient Low-Cost Memory Architecture for Interactive Ray Casting

This chapter presents a low-cost memory architecture running at 100 MHz which is suited for any PCI-based volume rendering accelerator using the ray-casting approach. By utilizing the features of current SDRAM technology, parallel access to all voxels required for trilinear interpolation, a cubic addressing scheme, and a buffering mechanism accommodating memory latency very efficient memory access and Volume data processing is achieved.

Volume Rendering is a computationally intensive process that requires a very large amount of data to be accessed putting a high demand on the memory interface. Similiar to polygon based hardware accelerators, the requirements for the memory interface are very high (even higher) and currently the ultimately limiting factor of any volume rendering accelerator. Nevertheless, while different memory architectures for ray-casting based volume rendering have been presented only a few have been described in detail or analyzed with respect to their feasibility and correct timing behavior.

In Verve, Knittel presented a memory interface that uses eight different memories, such that all eight voxels necessary for trilinear interpolation can be fetched in parallel [44]. A total of 16 SIMMs were estimated for a 512^3 dataset. Similar to Verve, VIRIM uses eight memory units to allow parallel access for each sample. Additionally, each unit contains two banks allowing for ping-pong readout. Although the authors refer to "data cubes", it is not clear whether a cubic addressing scheme, like the one presented here, is used or not.

The DIV^2A system, as proposed by Lichtermann, uses multiple image processors, each having its own private voxel memory [57]. To meet the timing of the processor's clock frequency, static memory is used and hence, no special memory architecture is necessary. However, this prevents the system from being considered as a low-cost volume rendering accelerator, feasible on a PCI card.

Knittel's VIZARD[45, 46] reduced memory bandwidth by using a Redundant Block Compression scheme. Additionally, an SRAM-based Cache which enabled the exploitation of ray-to-ray coherence was included. However, ray-to-ray coherence only improved the frame-rate for close-ups and fly-throughs and does not have as high a hit ratio as the caching scheme presented in this chapter.

A volume memory architecture based on RAMBUS DRAM was presented by de Boer et al.[13]. Similar to the VIRIM[33] system, volume data is distributed among eight memory units. Additionally, two or more SRAM caches are used for each memory unit (non-blocking caches). Depending on the size of the subcubes, the total cache size can range from 32 MByte to 100 MByte of SRAM. This is not feasible on a single PCI card, nor is it low-cost. RDRAM requires a special interface chip (ASIC) to accomodate the 400MHz or higher clock speed and non-standard signal voltages of RDRAM. Furthermore, for a true ray-casting accelerator, short transfers are frequent and this is handled very inefficiently by the RAMBUS protocol[61].

In [39] a cubic memory addressing scheme for access to 64 binary voxel values in parallel was presented. While the cubic addressing presented here is similar much larger voxel sizes such as 32bit and the use of modern memory devices such as SDRAM are now required to enable high quality images and interactivity.

Very recently and independently, a memory architecture similar to the one in Section 5.2.2 has been presented[82]. The architecture uses standard SDRAMs making use of the four internal banks. However, an accurate simulation and timing analysis has not been presented.

5.1   Memory Access

To describe and measure the performance of a memory architecture the addressing and behaviour of modern memory devices must be considered first. In this Section, we will first go through the use of SDRAMs for ray casting and propose a model that can be used for measuring an SDRAM's performance when used with an application that requires constant random access. We will then describe the cubic addressing scheme which uses a subcube as the basic unit of addressing, unlike traditional addressing schemes. The cubic addressing scheme will be extended to show the calculation of addresses when using eight parallel memory modules as shown in [44].

The advantages of SDRAM over several other types of memory, including RDRAM, is discussed in [61] where SDRAM is chosen due to it's cheap cost and availability. Since very short transfer sizes are also required here, SDRAM is still the perferred choice. Also RDRAM requires a custom ASIC to drive the 600MHz interface and this would be expensive and difficult to fit with other components on a PCI card.

5.1.1 SDRAM terminology

Interactive ray casting places very specialised demands on the use of SDRAMs and a clear model of SDRAM behaviour is necessary to correctly estimate performance. All SDRAM providers readily supply datasheets that reveal a varying range of information concerning their product. This information ranges from electrical specifications right through to command descriptions. Using the device datasheets and the requirements of our application we must determine the suitability and performance of the device.

The first restraint we have is that a new read command with a random address is sent to the SDRAM every clock cycle. This means that the SDRAM must be used with a burst length of one and therefore we cannot use one of the main features of SDRAMs which is the ability to issue precharge and bank select commands while long burst reads are in progress. We want to minimise these precharge and bank select commands since they represent an increase in the memory latency. To model the operation of a memory architecture and determine its performance given these constraints and limitations we have designed a simplified SDRAM state diagram shown in Figure 5.1.

The SDRAM state diagram focuses on read operations only and the delays experienced in consecutive reads. At power on, the SDRAM starts in the precharge state and moves to the idle state. To save precharge time, precharge is issued for all four banks and four registers are set to indicate all banks are precharged. When a bank activate is required a check is made on the bank's precharge register to see if the bank is precharged and and if so then an activate command can be issued without precharge. Once in the idle state a row activate command is issued to select a bank and row address followed by a read command which sends the column address to the SDRAM.

Before the next read, the memory controller checks its address and compares it to the previous read to check if a bank active or precharge is required. Firstly, the memory controller checks if the next read is within the currently active row and in this case another read is issued with the next address. In this chapter we will use the terms caches and pages to refer to the currently active row in one bank of an SDRAM. If it is not in the same row, then the appropriate bank will need to be activated. Before bank activation the memory controller checks the bank has been precharged, if not, a precharge will need to be issued otherwise the memory controller issues an activate command for that bank.

There are several other timing constraints that affect the bank switching time of an SDRAM. Firstly, an interleaved bank activate command cannot occur within a time period of t_{RRD}. The test for the number of reads in the previous bank ensures that this condition is met by adding a small delay if not enough time has passed while reading in the current bank. Two further conditions are the minimum time interval between successive bank activate commands to the same bank, t_{RC}, and the minimum time between an activate bank command and a precharge command t_{RAS}. These conditions can be met by adding delay time after the number of reads in the current bank is tested.

The perfomance and requirements of SDRAMs from different manufacturers can vary affecting the precharge times, bank switching times and other timing constraints. Figure 5.1 and the simulation results are based on the timing information for NEC 256Mbit 4 bank SDRAMs [66]. These were chosen because they have the fastest performance when continuous single reads are required. The timings are shown in Table 5.1. There are SDRAMs that run at speeds greater than 100MHz, but the SDRAMs performance will be limited by the board and its components onto which they are finally incorporated.

Parameter	Time (ns)
Clock cycle time	10
Precharge time, t_{RP}	20
Row Activate, t_{RCD}	20
Read data (CAS) latency, 2	20
Minimum Times	
Activate one to activate another, t_{RRD}	20
Activate one to activate same, t_{RC}	70
Activate to precharge, t_{RAS}	50

Table 5.1: Characteristics for NEC SDRAM

5.1.2   Cubic Addressing Scheme

The main difference between traditional addressing and the cubic addressing scheme is that the basic unit for address calculation is a s^3 sub-cube instead of a single voxel. Sub-cube addressing has been used previously in the field of parallel volume rendering[59, 68, 37]. However, in this algorithm voxels are grouped into sub-cubes which fit into a row of an SDRAM. A cubic address first divides the x, y and z coordinates by s to find the s^3 sub-cube that the voxel is in and then finds the modulus by s of the x, y and z coordinates to determine the voxel position within the s^3 sub-cube. The address, A, is calculated using the following set of equations :

$$A = s^3 A_C + A_V \qquad (5.1)$$

$$A_C = \lfloor \frac{V_x}{s} \rfloor + \frac{D_x}{s} \lfloor \frac{V_y}{s} \rfloor + \frac{D_x D_y}{s^2} \lfloor \frac{V_z}{s} \rfloor \qquad (5.2)$$

$$A_V = V_x \bmod s + s(V_y \bmod s) + s^2(V_z \bmod s) \qquad (5.3)$$

where,

A	is the cubic address,
A_C	is the address of the voxel's sub-cube,
A_V	is the voxel address inside the sub-cube,
s	is the size of the sub-cube,
V_x, V_y, and V_z	are the voxel coordinates,
D_x, D_y, and D_z	are the dimensions of the dataset.

If $s = 8$ and a cache size of 512 voxels is used, one sub-cube of 8^3 voxels is stored in the cache. Assuming the traditional method of calculating the address, A, is $x + ny + n^2 z$ is used and the cache is filled linearly then a ray travelling parallel to the x axis would only require a cache refresh at the beginning of the ray and have a 100% cache hit to miss ratio. But when the ray traces parallel to the z axis and a cache refresh is required for every trilinear neighbourhood read the cache is missed every time. When comparing cubic addressing to traditional memory addressing the cache results for ray casting along the x,y and z axes all have a 87.5% cache hit to miss ratio since every eighth voxel requires a cache refresh.

5.1.3   Parallel Memory Access

Figure 5.2 shows the arrangement of data in eight parallel memory modules. In Figure 5.2, MO to $M7$ represent the eight parallel memories and for each sample point each one of the eight parallel memories is required to deliver one voxel. If (V_x, V_y, V_z) is divisable by two then the coordinates used to calculate the address for each memory are the original coordinates divided by two. The calculation of the addresses becomes more complex when the sample point is between two neighbourhoods of the previously mentioned case. This is discussed in[44] and the base address of a neighbourhood is modified using an address modification unit (incrementer) before each memory bank. The combination here of both Cubic Addressing and Parallel Memory Access results in address modification affecting the calculation of both the sub-cube address and voxel address within the sub-cube. Therefore the recalculation of only the voxel coordinates for each parallel memory is presented.

For example, consider the set of new memory addresses for sample $S2$ compared to the addresses for sample $S1$, where samples are depicted as a cross marked on the ray in Figure 5.2. If $M0$ for sample $S1$ is the origin then all eight memory addresses are identical. But, the address calculations for sample $S2$ will result in new addresses for memories $M0$, $M1$, $M2$ and $M3$, while the addresses for memories $M4$, $M5$, $M6$ and $M7$ will remain the same.

When calculating the eight memory addresses for the current sample point, the sample address must first be divided by two before memory addresses are calculated (implemented as a shift operation), because each memory stores only every second voxel. For example, given that memory $M0$ is at the origin, for each memory address calculation the sample's x coordinate must be divided by two and the modulus by two of the x coordinate added to it. For memory $M1$ the sample's x coordinate only needs to be divided by two. The newly calculated coordinates to be used when calculating the address for each of the eight memories are as follows :

$$M_x = \frac{V_x}{2} + V_x \bmod 2 \tag{5.4}$$

$$M_y = \frac{V_y}{2} + V_y \bmod 2 \tag{5.5}$$

$$M_z = \frac{V_z}{2} + V_z \bmod 2 \tag{5.6}$$

$$U_x = \frac{V_x}{2} \quad U_y = \frac{V_y}{2} \quad U_z = \frac{V_z}{2} \tag{5.7}$$

$$M0 : (M_x, M_y, M_z) \quad M1 : (U_x, M_y, M_z)$$
$$M2 : (M_x, U_y, M_z) \quad M3 : (U_x, U_y, M_z)$$
$$M4 : (M_x, M_y, U_z) \quad M5 : (U_x, M_y, U_z)$$
$$M6 : (M_x, U_y, U_z) \quad M7 : (U_x, U_y, U_z)$$

5.1.4 Memory Access Buffering

Using the cubic addressing scheme described above, consider the situation when the ray in Figure 5.2 crosses the y-z plane of the next s^3 sub-cube of voxels and causes memories $M0$, $M2$, $M4$ and $M6$ to change their coordinates and refresh their cache with the values of the next s^3 sub-cube. At this point the memories $M1$, $M3$, $M5$ and $M7$ will not yet have left their current sub-cube of voxels and so have not had a cache refresh. If the individual memory cache refreshes described above happen in separate cycles of the pipeline, then the pipeline will have to stall twice. Once for the first four memories to refill their caches and also at a later time when the second four memories refill their caches. This is a simplified example and depending on the direction in which the ray crosses between sub-cubes a particular memory can have up to 2 cache misses consecutively. To minimise the effect of cache misses and subsequent pipeline stalling a FIFO buffer is introduced into a ray casting pipeline as shown in Figure 5.3.

With this buffering the only time the pipeline must stall is when the voxel FIFO of a particular memory is empty at the same time that this memory requires a cache refill. The frame time is now dependent on only the performance of the slowest SDRAM, whereas with unbuffered memory access the frame time is dependent on the sum of the slowest SDRAM access at every read of a trilinear neighbourhood.

5.2 Memory Architectures

The memory architecture chosen for implementation is dependent on a number of factors which are constantly changing given currently available technology. This section presents three memory architectures and shows the progression from solutions with optimal performance and poor feasibility to increased practicalility using four DIMMs and maintaining high performance.

5.2.1 Sixty Four Memories

An ideal solution for an arbitrary, but conflict free memory access without any danger of pipeline stalls is the use of 64 independantly accessible SDRAMs. For simplicity, the principle idea is depicted in 2D with 16 SDRAMs in Figure 5.4. The four currently accessed SDRAMs are highlighted (0,1,2,3). Ensuring there is no access penalty while crossing a page boundary, the 2×2 Neigborhoods across the page boundary have to be in four of the other 12 SDRAMs not currently accessed. SDRAMs 4-15 can be precharged and activated while accessing SDRAMs 1-4, so the new voxels are available within the next clock cycle when crossing the page boundary. This configuration works for two principal axes directions, with 64 SDRAMs, it can be extended for accesses along all three principal axes directions, no matter if we use cubic addressing or not. While giving us the fastest possible access time, this solution has a severe limitation. It requires the calculation and distribution of 64 independant addresses which is expensive to build and exceeds the board space budget for a PCI-Card by far.

One alternative is to simply use 8 SDRAMs, which is the minimum required to fetch a trilinear interpolation subcube with one memory access. While this is more likely to fit on a PCI board, the solution suffers from unbalanced access times and a smaller solution is possible if we employ the banks in SDRAMs.

5.2.2 Eight Logical Memories

By taking advantage of the shorter switching times between banks in modern SDRAMs, a near optimal and more practical solution using eight logical memory banks can be used. If we take the row size of one bank of a SDRAM and place the neighbouring subcubes in the x,y and z directions into neighbouring SDRAM banks we can place three into the same SDRAM and use a second SDRAM to provide four more banks for the remaining neighbouring subcubes, assuming 4 banks per SDRAM. This results in another level of cubic hierarchy in the memory architecture. If we want to have 32 bits per voxel as proposed in the original VIZARDII[63] design then two 16bit wide devices will be required per logical memory. The resulting layout of the memory architecture and the positioning of SDRAM banks in the dataset's coordinates is shown in Figure 5.5. When a ray passes into the neighbourhood of the eight banks a precharge is issued across all eight banks so that a switch between banks will only take as much time as a bank activate instead of a precharge and activate command. This design means that the same results can be expected in each of the three principal axes directions. Using the distance between voxels in the original dataset the effective size of each individual bank, A - H in Figure 5.5, is 16^3 and the size of the cube between precharge commands is now 32^3.

Vetterman et. al.[82] plan to build exactly this memory structure for their new interactive volume rendering architecture. However, an important consideration when building any hardware accelerator is the maximum speed of the system and effectively the speed that the memory can operate at. We would prefer to make use of low cost off-the-shelf memory boards and maintain a system clock of 100MHz by having a simpler overall design.

5.2.3 Four DIMMs

When considering the previously presented memory architectures, it is apparent that favourable access times can be achieved by exploiting the SDRAM caches to store large voxel neighborhoods. However, for a low-cost single PCI board solution, these architectures are not well suited.

Targeting low-cost, makes the use of standard off-the-shelf components mandatory. Dual In-line Memory Modules (DIMMs) are readily available, extremely cheap, and in daily use. Another advantage is that DIMMs can easily be exchanged allowing for "upgradability" of the memory. However, aiming for a single PCI board solution constrains the possible implementation. In discussions with industrial partners it has become clear that more than four DIMMs is not realistic for a single PCI board solution. A memory architecture using four DIMMs is shown in Figure 5.6.

Using only four DIMM modules limits the number of individual memory addresses. Hence, fetching the eight voxels—required for trilinear interpolation—in parallel, is only feasible using either two cycles (as presented in [63]) or by replicating data. The memory addresses used to fetch a trilinear neighbourhood using four DIMMs in shown in Figure 5.7 Although data replication is not a desirable solution, the feasibility means that it is an acceptable trade off. Furthermore, DIMM modules are relatively inexpensive, for example, a dataset of 512^3 voxels with eight bit data stored using data replication would be in the range of a few hundred US$.

As a result of the data replication, we need to store two consecutive voxels instead of one. This means an addressing scheme where only four addresses are calculated is required. These four addresses are the same as those presented in Section 5.1.3 and will be addresses $M0 - M3$ when the z coordinate is divisable by two and $M4 - M7$ when it is not. Additionally, only four internal banks per

SDRAM on the DIMM are available (A-D), and hence, the voxel neighborhood contained over all caches of all memory devices is reduced by 50% compared to the previous architecture. This increases the number of bank activates and precharge commands therefore reducing the average access-time. However, as is shown in Section 5.3, this reduction has hardly any impact on the frame-rate, due to the relatively large page caches.

5.3   Results

To show the benefits of using buffered memory accessing and determine the performance difference between the presented memory architectures (sixty four memories, eight logical memories, and four DIMMs), a software simulation was used to determine timings using the SDRAM model as described in Section 5.1.1 was applied.

To gain a good perspective on the performance that a system would give, the results have been averaged over a set of twenty representative views. The views are rendered with their view direction determined by the center point of each triangle in an icosahedron centered around the dataset. Furthermore, all measurements have been performed on a total of three different datasets, which are:

Foot: This is a CT scan of the front part of a human foot with 256^3 voxels. Images of this dataset are given in Figure 5.8(a). Two different materials can be classified; Bone and flesh.

Arteries: CT angiography has been used as the acquisition device to generate this dataset of 256^3 voxels. A single material – the blood vessels of one half of the human brain – can be classified, see Images in Figure 5.8(b).

Statue: The foot of a bronze statue has been scanned, resulting in a dataset of $341^2 \times 91$ voxels with a non uniform spacing of $1, 1, 0.25$. Up to four materials can be classified; Bronze, an iron cylinder which is behind the foot, resin, and plaster. Images of this dataset are shown in Figure 5.8(c).

For each presented memory architecture, measurements have been performed casting 256^2 rays onto each of the datasets using perspective projection. As a result, an average frame rate, average memory access time, and cache hit ratio have been calculated using the twenty views, as mentioned above. The results of these measurements are shown in Table 5.2.

Dataset	Memory Type	Av. FPS Early Ray Termination		Av. Time (ns)		Cache hits	Image
		Buffered	Unbuffered	Buffered	Unbuffered		
CT foot	Sixty Four Memories	12.3	12.3	10	10	100	5.8(a)(b)
	Eight Logical Memories	11.0	8.3	11.2	14.9	95.3	
	Four DIMMs	9.7	8.4	12.7	14.7	90.7	
Arteries	Sixty Four Memories	10.6	10.6	10	10	100	5.8(c)
	Eight Logical Memories	9.5	7.2	11.2	14.8	95.3	
	Four DIMMs	8.4	7.2	12.7	14.7	90.8	
Statue 1	Sixty Four Memories	7.4	7.4	10	10	100	5.8(e)
	Eight Logical Memories	6.7	5.1	11.2	14.7	95.4	
	Four DIMMs	5.9	5.1	12.6	14.6	91.1	
Statue 2	Sixty Four Memories	5.0	5.0	10	10	100	5.8(f)
	Eight Logical Memories	4.8	4.1	10.6	12.4	97.6	
	Four DIMMs	4.5	4.1	11.3	12.4	95.4	
256^3	Sixty Four Memories	9.8	9.8	10	10	100	
	Eight Logical Memories	8.7	6.6	11.2	14.8	95.4	
	Four DIMMs	7.7	6.6	12.7	14.7	90.9	

Table 5.2: Memory timing for three different datasets.

On average, the number of frames per second achievable if in each voxel neighbourhood a sample is generated—assuming a 256^3 dataset—is 5 for buffered memory and 4 for unbuffered memory. However, due to early ray termination and perspective projection much higher frame rates can be achieved, except the worst case where all voxels values are classified semi-transparent, thus preventing any early ray termination at all. Fortunately, for most application fields, this happens rarely. Overall, this frame rate gives an upper bound to the number of samples possibly being generated per second. The last row of the table using 256^3 samples shows frames per second of 7 for buffered and 6 for unbuffered where the speed up is due only to the reduction in the number of samples due to perspective projection.

The buffered accessing scheme as presented in Section 5.1.4 performs very well, as shown in Table 5.2. For all datasets, the average access time is reduced and hence more samples can be generated which adds between two and four more frames per second. The Four DIMMs architecture doesn't need buffering in z direction, therefore buffering does not improve frame-rates as much as for the eight logical memories. In the above described case, where in each sample neighbourhood a sample is generated, the access buffering increases the frame rate by 20%.

An advantage of the memory architectures are the caches once applying over-sampling. In general, higher sampling rates along the cast rays decrease the average frame rate according to the oversampling rate. At the same time, the average access time to the SDRAMs is decreased because more samples occur within the same cache. This increases the overall cache hit ratio and hence, the frame rate is not reduced by 50% but only by 40%, as it can be seen in Table 5.2 (Statue 1 and Statue 2). The average cache hit ratio increases from approximately 90% to 95% while at the same time reducing the impact of the access buffering scheme.

As expected, the non feasible memory architecture using sixty four memories always reaches the optimum of 10 ns and a 100% cache hit ratio. However, the difference between the results for the four DIMMs and eight logical memories is always less than 1 frame per second. As it can be seen, the four DIMMs architecture can be used with virtually no loss in performance but large gains in practicality, implementability and upgradeability, thus enabling a single PCI board solution running at full 100MHz.

5.4 Summary

This chapter presented a low-cost memory architecture based on off-the-shelf DIMM modules running at 100 MHz. Using parallel accesses, a cubic addressing scheme, FIFOs accomodating memory latency, and data replication, high frame-rates are achieved. Averaged over a set of representative views, up to 9Hz can be achieved. Using such an onboard memory interface makes ray-to-ray coherence caches – as presented in [46, 63] – redundant. The presented memory architecture is used in the VIZARDII system presented in Chapter 9.

So far, early ray termination has been applied as the only algorithmic optimization. However space leaping, as presented in Chapter 7, can greatly increase the frame-rate by skipping homogeneous areas. An interesting subject of future research is how to make use of SDRAM burst mode to hide precharge and bank switching delays for ray casting based volume rendering architectures.

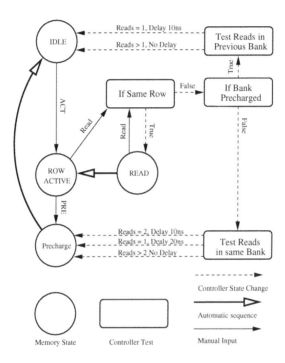

Figure 5.1: Simplified SDRAM State Diagram for continuous reads with burst length 1 and absolute values based on NEC SDRAM.

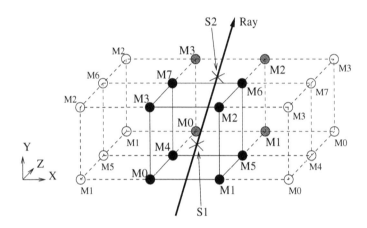

Figure 5.2: The positioning of voxels in eight parallel memory banks and two sample points along a ray.

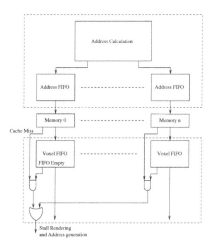

Figure 5.3: The FIFO buffers for addresses and voxel values.

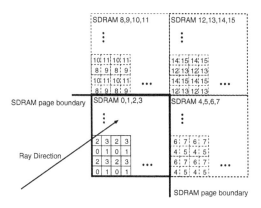

Figure 5.4: Memory access across page boundaries with 64 SDRAMs. Interpolation neigborhoods consist of 2 × 2 squares, the numbers denote SDRAM delivering the voxel.

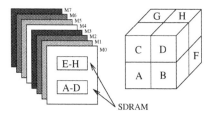

Figure 5.5: Memory architecture using 8 logical memories.

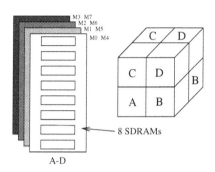

Figure 5.6: Memory architecture using 4 DIMMs.

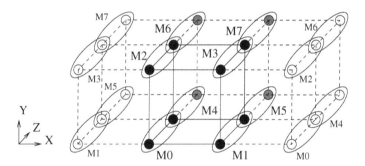

Figure 5.7: The addressing values for voxels in the four DIMMs memory architectre. Address value Mn is sent to DIMM (n mod 4).

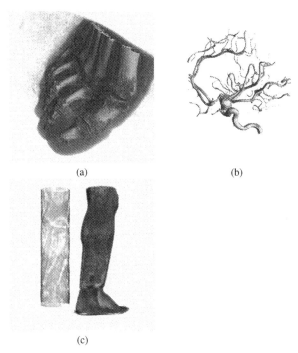

(a)   (b)

(c)

Figure 5.8: (a) A CT scan of a human food. (b)A CT angiography scan of human brain vessels. (c) The foot from a statue casting.

Chapter 6

Ray Queueing and Sorting for Ray Casting Hardware

This chapter presents a hardware design that processes several rays simultaneously to improve the memory access and compositing performance for three dimensional image synthesis using ray casting. By processing multiple rays the memory access coherence of a group of neighbouring rays can be exploited and fewer page misses in a modern SDRAM memory device are encountered. Tracing multiple rays also avoids the data hazard that occurs when tracing the path of a single ray. Implementation of the presented design in a real time volume rendering system improves the performance of the system by increasing the number of frames rendered per second.

The standard approach to ray casting is to follow the path of each ray to completion before starting a subsequent ray. This results in memory paging as the first ray is traced and further memory paging delays as subsequent rays are traced. The performance can be improved by tracing a group of rays together with the endpoint or tip of the rays within close proximity. This will effectively reduce the amount of paging by the number of rays traced together.

Vettermann et al.[82] suggest to solve the data hazard problem using a ray queue and also discuss the memory benefits of tracing several rays together. This chapter also presents a design that makes use of a ray queue but it ensures memory coherence is achieved by comparing final memory address values.

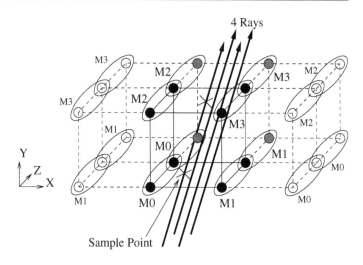

Figure 6.1: Four rays and associated voxels showing relevant memories.

6.1 Multiple Rays

To improve the performance of ray casting multiple rays can be cast at the same time through a dataset as shown with four rays in Figure 6.1. Figure 6.1 shows a sample point taken along one ray with the closest eight voxels making up its voxel neighbourhood emphasised as black filled circles. This voxel neighbourhood must be read from memory and trilinearly interpolated to calculate the new value, called the sample, at that sample point. In Figure 6.1 the memory modules that the voxels will be read from are indicated by Mn, where n is the memory module number. To read the eight values four memories each provide two values. When tracing multiple rays it is important to keep the current sample along each ray within close proximity of the current samples on the other rays to ensure memory addresses are similar. If one ray advances beyond the other rays then every time voxels are read from memory for the advanced ray a page fault will occur and the ray casting will stall during memory row active and precharge time.

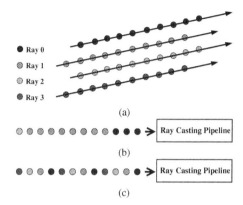

(a)

(b)

(c)

Figure 6.2: A group of four rays showing the sample points along each ray (a), sample processing order when each ray is processed individually (b) and when tracing four interleaved rays (c).

Figure 6.2 illustrates the order in which the samples of the four rays shown in (a) are input into the ray-casting pipeline for processing one ray at a time (b), or interleaving the processing of four rays (c).

The ray casting approach to Volume Rendering can be broken down into a pipeline of operations. The main stages of ray casting are the Ray Setup, Ray Incrementor, Trilinear Interpolation, Shading and Compositing calculation stages as shown in Figure 6.3(a). When distance coding is used to speed up ray casting the distance value is sent from Memory to the Ray Incrementor as shown in the figure. The Compositing stage calculates the final pixel values that make up the screen image by reading the pixel values and compositing new shaded samples with the pixel. These two feedback loops represent potential data hazards that will cause empty cycles to be propergated through the pipeline.

Between these main stages several further pipeline stages are added to improve performance and to complete the pipeline as shown in Figure 6.3(b). First a Ray Queue for storing the current position of more than one ray, and then stages for Address Calculation and an SDRAM Controller are added as required to interface to the memory. An additional Address FIFO and Voxel FIFO improves memory

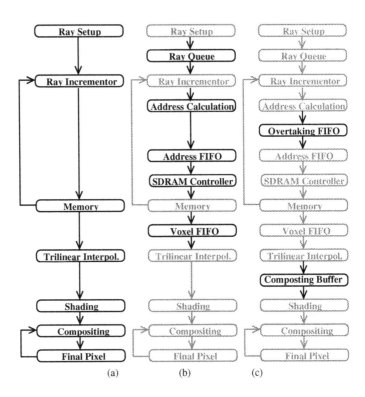

Figure 6.3: The calculation stages in a ray casting pipeline.

performance by allowing different memories to change pages at different times as described in Chapter 5. The new pipeline stages between Ray Increment and the Memory represent a latency of 6. This latency means that when distance coding is used the pipeline is empty until a distance value is returned by the memory. This problem is avoided by the introduction of the Ray Queue which passes the address for more than one ray at a time allowing the pipeline to calculate other ray data while it waits for the distance value from memory. But using a Ray Queue introduces the problem that the other rays may change the current cache page in the memory and stall the entire pipeline more frequently than with only a single ray.

To minimise the memory stalling effects when using several rays an *Overtaking FIFO* is introduced as shown in Figure 6.3(c). The Overtaking FIFO reorders the memory addresses in order to minimise page changes in the memory. A *Compositing Buffer* is also introduced to correctly sort the samples calculated for the Shading and Compositing stages and to eliminate the poor compositing performance of a single ray.

6.2   Overtaking FIFOs

An Overtaking FIFO takes address values as input and reorders the addresses so that consecutive addresses read from the FIFO are the most similar. The architecture of an Overtaking FIFO with 4 registers is shown in Figure 6.4. In Figure 6.4 the *Compare* unit is responsible for comparing the incoming address and addresses in the first three FIFOs with that of the last FIFO, the address being read out. The address that is the closest match to the out going address is promoted to the last register, therefore the value entering the FIFO can overtake the values in the FIFO and be entered into the final register instead of the first. The depth of the Overtaking FIFO is determined by the maximum number of rays supported by the Ray Queue.

To determine whether two address values are within the same memory page their address values must be compared. The Address Calculation unit generates four address values for four separate DIMM memory modules as described in Chapter 5. Each address value is 22 bits wide and comparing 4 of these values would be an expensive computation. To reduce this computation we only consider the octant that the address' sample point is currently residing in reducing the number of bits for comparison to 3. The four octant values for the incoming and first three registers are compared to the octant values of the outgoing register for

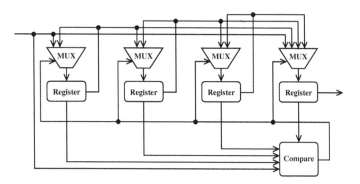

Figure 6.4: The architecture of the Overtaking FIFO.

equivalence. The number of equivalent octant values is counted and then the totals sorted. The address with the highest number of equivalent octants is then placed in the final register and all other registers are advanced or stalled accordingly.

A more complex comparison would be to compare all values in the FIFO with each other and sort the addresses based on coherence. This would increase the complexity and reduce the scalability of the design and not improve the performance. Comparison to the outgoing address already ensures that two consecutive addresses have maximum coherence. Another possible alternative is to increment the address of the first ray in the Ray Queue while it is in the current memory page before moving to the next ray in the queue. This would mean the Ray Incrementor would have to wait until address calculation was completed to make such a comparison slowing the pipeline substantially.

6.3 Compositing Buffer

The second data hazard in the Ray Casting pipeline is at the compositing stage. It is possible that a single ray will produce address values so that even with multiple rays the only values going to the compositor are from the same ray. The compositing requires a multiplication of the current value with the previous value and cannot start a new multiplication until the current one is completed. To achieve a high clock speed most multiplier designs are pipelined. The 12-bit multiplier used in the VIZARDII compositing engine is broken into 4 stages and slows the speed of the system by a factor of four as the new result waits for the current calculation to complete. By introducing the Ray Queue and the Compositing Buffer it is possible to remove this delay and improve performance by a factor of four. This is done by sorting the sample values from the Trilinear Interpolation according to their original ray number. The compositing unit then proceeds by reading the data from ray 1 through to ray 4 before reading from ray 1 again filling the compositing pipeline.

6.4 Results

To measure the performance improvement expected from the Overtaking Fifos, the results have been simulated and averaged over a set of twenty representative views. The views are rendered with their view direction determined by the center point of each triangle in an icosahedron centered around the dataset. Measurements have been performed casting 256^2 rays onto a 256^3 CT angiography datasets using perspective projection. The Rendering Fifos improved performance for average memory access time from 12.7 ns to 12.3 ns which equates to an improvement for average frame rate from 8.0 fps to 8.3 fps. The improvement is over an ideal compositor which does not take into account the 4 cycle latency required for compositing.

The compositing buffer provides a 4 times speedup in performance by allowing the system to use a 4 stage multiplier running at clock speeds of around 100MHz in the compositing stage. The combination of the Ray Queue, Overtaking FIFO and Compositing Buffer enable the use of a fully pipelined compositor resulting in a significant performance improvement.

6.5 Summary

This chapter presented a new design for using ray queueing in ray casting architectures that overcomes the problems of reduced memory performance and compositing hazards by introducing two new pipeline stages. The design improves performance by eliminating the data hazard of compositing a single ray by introducing multiple rays and sorting them to improve memory performance. This design is implemented in the VIZARDII system as presented in Chapter 9.

Chapter 7

Sub-cube based Space Leaping for Ray Casting Hardware

This chapter presents a fast, easily implemented technique for improving the performance of ray casting systems implemented in hardware. Space leaping is a technique where the empty space in Volume data is skipped over instead of every sample being calculated. This skipping of empty space can have a significant effect on the performance of ray casting. An occupancy map that indicates empty and non-empty sub-cubes of a volume dataset is used which is small and can be easily stored on-chip for hardware implementations.

The VIZARD architecture presented by Knittel[46] used an octant based distance coding scheme that skipped empty octants by storing the multiple of the increment vector in empty voxel blocks. The size of these octants was limited and the performance of the entire system was limited by memory access of the Volume data from main memory via the PCI bus.

Vettermann et al.[82] proposed a ray casting architecture which can integrate algorithmic optimizations such as early ray termination and space leaping, hiding most of the latency. In this architecture, an additional distance volume is used to store the Euclidean distance to the closest contributing voxel. Memory access latency is high because the distance volume is stored in SDRAM. This is circumvented by interleaving the processing of multiple rays. However, this significantly aggravates the task of coordinating the memory accesses and requires a significant amount of logic for implementation. Furthermore, once a certain threshold of remaining rays is reached, stall cycles are introduced.

The proposed RACE architecture[75] exploits early ray termination and estimates real-time frame-rates for parallel and perspective projection. Space leaping capabilities have not yet been integrated but the authors state that succeeding architectures will include this and an acceleration of a factor of two is expected[75].

These two architectures require an entire distance volume to be pre-computed[46] and stored[82]. Generally, the generation of distance volumes has been widely investigated for CSG [7], volume rendering [81, 94], haptics in volume rendering [31], iso-surface extraction [43] and others. However, the computational costs are not neglectable and for 8 bit distance and voxel values, the memory requirements are doubled which is impractical for larger volumes.

Amanatides[1] presents an algorithm for fast and simple sub-cube traversal for ray-tracing. This algorithm is used to determine the current sub-cube that the ray is passing through and does not calculate the sampling positions along a ray as needed for ray casting.

The algorithm presented in this chapter does not require an entire distance volume, has a straight forward, low logic usage hardware implementation

This chapter presents the possible integration of this method into the VIZARD II architecture. However, occupancy maps can easily be integrated into other ray casting architectures, i.e. [82] and possibly [72].

7.1   Space leaping algorithm

Ray casting using space leaping is performed by advancing the ray to the next sample point of interest instead of incrementing the ray's current sample position by a small increment. In this technique only sub-cubes of empty space are skipped, thus the complexity of precomputation is significantly reduced. The algorithm also calculates a conservatively estimated distance to the next sample point within the next sub-cube, if the current sub-cube is empty.

7.1.1   Space Leaping Algorithm

Initially, the sub-cubes of interest within the dataset are mapped by calculating a small occupancy map containing a single bit per sub-cube of the volume dataset. The bit indicates whether a sub-cube is empty or contains data requiring sampling. This leads to a very space efficient discretized representation of the volume, i.e. for a 256^3 volume and sub-cubes of 16^3 voxels, a total of 4 Kbits of memory is required. In Figure 7.1, a simple example of an occupancy map is given for the two dimensional case.

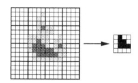

Figure 7.1: The Space Leap Volume for the 2D case.

For each sample along the ray, the corresponding bit in the occupancy map is checked using the upper address bits of the sample position. If the entry in the occupancy map indicates a non-empty sub-cube, sampling along the ray is simply continued. Otherwise, this sub-cube will be skipped by a distance, conservatively approximated to the first sample within the subsequent sub-cube by adding the increment vector multiplied by the amount of samples to be skipped. The number

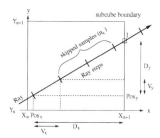

Figure 7.2: Calculation of the skipping

n_s of samples the ray may skip can be calculated by dividing the distance from the actual ray position to the intersection point (I_x, I_y, I_z) of the ray with the next sub-cube boundary by the length of one ray increment:

$$n_s = \left\lceil \frac{\sqrt{(I_x - P_x)^2 + (I_y - P_y)^2 + (I_z - P_z)^2}}{\sqrt{V_x^2 + V_y^2 + V_z^2}} \right\rceil \qquad (7.1)$$

with (P_x, P_y, P_z) being the actual ray position and V_x, V_y and V_z the ray increment in the corresponding direction, as shown in Figure 7.2 for the x coordinate. Since this involves the calculation of two Euclidean distances, which would be extremely expensive, a simpler approach was chosen for implementation.

The same result can be obtained if the relative distance to the boundaries in x, y and z direction is calculated. The minimum value determines the amount of steps that have to be taken to reach into the next sub-cube.

$$n_s = \min \left\{ \left\lceil \frac{D_x}{V_x} \right\rceil, \left\lceil \frac{D_y}{V_y} \right\rceil, \left\lceil \frac{D_z}{V_z} \right\rceil \right\} \qquad (7.2)$$

In order to increase the space leaping efficiency even further, a second level of hierarchy can be added. The entries of eight neighboring sub-cubes ($2 \times 2 \times 2$) can be grouped into an eight bit entry in the occupancy map. When all eight entries are zero (the entire byte is zero), the whole group of sub-cubes may be skipped, achieving a higher space leaping efficiency since more samples can be skipped in less cycles.

Generally, using the above described space leaping algorithm does not require any voxel to be accessed as long as samples along the ray are "taken" in empty sub-cubes. Thus, frequent swapping of memory pages due to rays stepping once in a sub-cube and skipping to the next sub-cube, is prevented increasing the overall memory utilization significantly.

7.2   Hardware implications

The additional costs in terms of computational hardware to implement the space leaping algorithm are quite modest. This section presents the hardware units required to calculate the increment when skipping a sub-cube and introducing ray queueing into the ray casting pipeline to handle the latency of the increment calculations. The advantage of multiple rays is that it also allows for high performance compositing to be implemented.

7.2.1   Space Leaping Hardware

To avoid calculating the exact distance in 3D space, we only calculate the relative distance along each axis as described in the previous section. The pipeline for computing the new increment used if a sub-cube is skipped is shown in Figure 7.3. The first operation in the pipeline involves finding the integer distance to the next

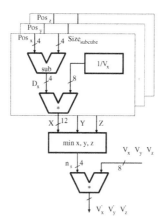

Figure 7.3: Pipeline for the skip calculator.

sub-cube. If we use 16^3 sub-cubes, a four bit subtraction is necessary to calculate each of D_x, D_y and D_z.

The second operation is to divide D_x, D_y and D_z by the ray increments V_x, V_y and V_z. To reduce the complexity of this division, we can pre-calculate the inverse of the V_x, V_y and V_z values once per ray and store the values, or store a larger adaptive division table covering the entire range of possible ray increment values. The division is then calculated by multiplying D_x, D_y and D_z by the pre-calculated $1/V_x, 1/V_y$ and $1/V_z$ value. This multiplier does not require a very high precision since we only compare its result with the results from the other relative directional increments to determine the minimum number of samples the ray may skip n_s. As long as the value is rounded down to the nearest integer, we might step a slightly shorter number of steps, slowing the overall ray casting marginally but reducing the size and latency of this multiplier.

The results from each component are then compared to determine the minimum number of steps n_s, which is then multiplied by the actual increment V along the ray. This second multiplier must have at least the same precision as the increment value, or rounding errors and possible image artifacts will result. We have found that with increment values with only 6-bit precision, image artifacts are present, so at least an 8-bit precision for the increment value is required. The newly calculated increment value is then added to the current address.

At the same time as the new increment value is calculated, the decision whether to skip the data is looked up from a small SRAM containing the occupancy map. If the sub-cube is to be skipped, then a mux selects the newly calculated increment value or the original increment value and sends it to the Ray Queue.

The occupancy map can be easily recalculated by the VIZARD II ray casting architecture by scanning over the entire volume. The VIZARD II architecture provides an extremely high memory bandwidth capable of scanning a 256^3 dataset in 20 ms[1], allowing interactive control of transfers functions to work with the space leaping hardware. Scanning for voxels = 0 can be performed during download of the volume, as the data will pass through the Xilinx FPGA, which can compute the occupancy mask as the download proceeds. A possible extension is to store multiple occupancy maps, one based on skipping voxels = 0 and others based on different classifications.

The logic to implement the skip calculator described above requires 124 CLB slices of a Xilinx Virtex XCV1000 FPGA, utilizing 1 % of the FPGA logic, not counting the required memory[2]. The clock frequency of the resulting pipeline is well above 100 Mhz and adds 8 cycles of latency to the address computation. Therefore, the processing of eight or more rays will be sufficient to accommodate latency.

7.2.2   Multiple Rays

The latency introduced by calculating the new skip increment means that if only one ray is processed the pipeline will stall, waiting for the calculation of the new skip distance to complete. To avoid this latency and maintain a full ray casting pipeline, we trace the path of more than one ray at a time. An example of four rays and their location relative to the memory banks used in the VIZARD II architecture is shown in Figure 7.4. A sample point taken along one ray is marked by an $\times$ and the closest eight voxels making up its voxel neighborhood are emphasized as black filled circles. This voxel neighborhood must be read from memory and trilinearly interpolated to calculate the new value, called the sample, at that

---

[1]The memory of the VIZARD II architecture is eight times interleaved. Hence, a volume dataset of 16 Msamples read from 100MHz SDRAM can be scanned 50 times per second.

[2]The occupancy map can be implemented using some of the 131 Kbits of on-chip Block SRAM of the Xilinx Virtex XCV1000 FPGA.

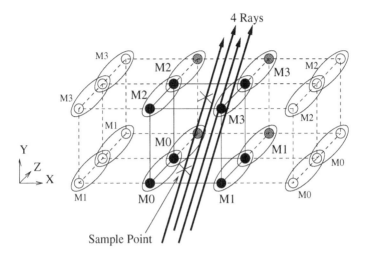

Figure 7.4: Four rays and associated voxels showing relevant memories.

sample point. The memory system of the VIZARD II board is described in detail in Chapter 5.

The main pipeline stages required for ray casting are shown in Figure 7.5(a). For space leaping a *Ray Queue* and it *Skip Calculator* must be added. In Figure 7.5, we also add stages for Address Calculation and SDRAM Control, as required to interface to the memory.

A *Compositing Buffer* is also introduced to correctly sort the samples for use in the Shading and Compositing stages.

7.2.3   Compositing Latency

Using a ray casting pipeline that processes only a single ray means that the compositing stage is required to perform a multiplication of the current value with the previous value. It cannot start a new multiplication until the current one is completed. Therefore the pipeline will have to stall until the complete compositing operation is completed, typically around 4 stages. Using the Compositing Buffer it is possible to remove this delay by interleaving processing of multiple rays in the compositing unit. This solves the compositing latency problem which would otherwise result in the operating frequency being reduced by a factor of four.

7.3 Results

A software simulation of the above described algorithm was used to measure the quantitative performance gains by counting the number of cycles needed per frame. Rather than using the software simulation of the VIZARDII architecture, the results could have beed recorded using measurements from the VHDL simulation of the ray casting pipeline. However, the hardware simulation takes 36 hours to render a 256^3 dataset.

For the evaluation of the described space leaping approach, we carefully selected a set of five different real-world datasets which are described in Table 7.1. The first two datasets are both simulation data, but the number of occupied vox-

Dataset	Size	Source	Occupied voxels
fuel	64^3	simulation	5,24 %
neghip	64^3	simulation	46,38 %
foot	256^3	CT-anio	28,94 %
skull	256^3	CT	88,42 %
vessel	256^3	CT-anio	1,01 %

Table 7.1: Set of datasets which have been used to evaluate the space leaping approach.

els varies significantly. The other three are scanned datasets. The skull is a very compact block of occupied voxels and due to noise, only a few unoccupied voxels—further-on referred to as empty voxels—exist. In contrast, the vessel dataset contains narrow structures which are present across the entire dataset but a large number of voxels is empty since there is almost no noise present. Finally, the foot dataset is a relatively compact block of occupied voxels with a moderate amount of noise. Figure 7.3 presents images of these datasets; for each dataset, there is one image showing all data present and another image where a classification revealing the important content has been applied.

7.3.1 Dataset characteristics

The percentage of empty voxels is given in Table 7.1, but does not reveal any estimate of the potential gain that can be expected from the presented space leaping mechanism. The potential benefit depends on the distribution of the empty voxels within sub-cubes. Therefore the amount of skipable sub-cubes was measured, using different sub-cube sizes ranging from 2^3 to 64^3 for each dataset. The results of these measurements are shown in Figure 7.7. Obviously, the smaller the sub-cubes, the higher the percentage of skipable sub-cubes. For the fuel datasets, no gain is achieved for sub-cubes of 32^3 and larger, since the fuel stream is concentric and symmetric such that all 32^3 sub-cubes always contain occupied voxels. For the neghip dataset, this already applies for sub-cubes of 16^3 and larger since the data is much more distributed over the entire grid. For the skull dataset the percentage of skipable sub-cubes is close to zero. This is due to the present noise which prevents any classification independent space leaping mechanism. The foot dataset is also noisy, but the noise is mostly around the tissue of the foot itself, which leaves many sub-cubes empty. Finally, the vessel dataset has a large amount of skipable sub-cubes, despite the fact that the arteries are present across the entire volume. The larger the sub-cubes, the lower the percentage of non-contributing sub-cubes. However, for each sub-cube at least one sample needs to be processed. Therefore, space leaping performance is better for larger sub-cube sizes.

Generally, classification is used to remove noise and other structures which are not of interest. We therefore used transfer functions visualizing the important content in each dataset. Images resulting from these transfer functions are given in Figure 7.3. Furthermore, Figure 7.8 illustrates the percentage of skipable voxels making use of these transfer functions. For the fuel and the neghip dataset, the percentage of non-skipable sub-cubes can be further reduced by 50%. Additionally, for the neghip 25% of sub-cubes of size 16^3 can now be skipped. The foot and the skull are the two datasets gaining the most; the percentage of non-skipable sub-cubes drops by a factor of 2 to 5. Overall, while for sub-cubes of size 2^3 more than 85% of all sub-cubes are empty, this does not translate into the best space leaping efficiency, which is elaborated in the next section.

As mentioned earlier, the occupancy map is stored in an on-chip storage (SRAM), to keep latency during the space leaping process as small as possible. Unfortunately, the capacity of this type of memory is limited, which puts an upper bound on the size of the feasible occupancy map. Table 7.2 illustrates the amount of memory needed for different dataset and sub-cube sizes. For the selected datasets,

Volume size/	64^3	128^3	256^3
Sub-cube size	[256 KBytes]	[2 MBytes]	[16 MBytes]
2^3	32 Kbits	256 Kbits	2 Mbits
4^3	**4 Kbits**	32 Kbits	256 Kbits
8^3	512 bits	**4 Kbits**	32 Kbits
16^3	64 bits	512 bits	**4 Kbits**
32^3	8 bits	64 bits	512 bits

Table 7.2: Storage needed for the space leap map.

4 Kbits offer a good percentage of skipable sub-cubes compared to the memory size. However, this may change for larger datasets (512^3), where one might achieve better results using 32 Kbit, which is still feasible.

7.3.2 Experiments and Discussion

The percentage of skipable sub-cubes does not exhibit the actual performance gains. What determines the optimal sub-cube size is given by the compactness of the structure(s) contained in the dataset and how much skipable space is around. Performance gains are generally limited to those parts of rays, which pass through empty sub cubes. For a thorough analysis, we generated animations of 72 frames for all five datasets rotating around the center of the dataset starting with the views given in Figure 7.3. For each frame, we accurately measured the number of cycles needed for image generation. These measurements include cycles for:

1. Taking all samples along all rays.

2. Applying early ray termination (ERT)

3. Applying space leaping additional to ERT, using sub-cube sizes ranging from 4^3 to 32^3.

The results are shown in Figure 7.3.2 where the graphs illustrate the view and classification dependent performance. To better comprehend the information of Figure 7.3.2, we translated it into frame-rates using the average memory access time of 12.5 nsecs per voxel. The results are shown in Table 7.3. In Table 7.3 the frame-rates are averaged over 72 frames (see Figure 7.3.2), acceleration *none*

Acceleration		none	ERT	4^3	8^3	16^3	32^3
fuel	'0'	16.1	16.4	27.3	41.9	45.8	16.4
	class	16.1	16.3	28.4	47.3	45.2	16.3
neghip	'0'	18.6	23.7	28.1	27.9	23.7	23.7
	class	18.6	23.3	36.2	46.2	31.5	23.3
foot	'0'	4.4	5.3	7.3	7.7	7.1	6.5
	class	4.4	5.3	9.0	14.4	19.1	16.8
skull	'0'	4.3	8.2	8.2	8.2	8.2	8.2
	class	4.3	7.8	12.9	17.3	16.0	10.8
vessel	'0'	4.3	4.7	7.8	10.4	10.7	8.3
	class	4.3	4.6	8.0	13.3	17.3	12.0

Table 7.3: Frame-rates for the five datasets when skipping empty voxels only ('0') and when exploiting the given classification (class).

stands for processing all samples along all rays and *ERT* stands for early ray termination. Generally, early ray termination is not a very efficient acceleration technique, unless the viewpoint is close to a highly opaque object covering large areas of the screen-space. For the presented views, performance gains vary from almost zero for the fuel dataset to 25% for the neghip dataset. The only exception is the skull dataset, where a 90% performance is gained due to the opaque skull.

Space leaping based on skipping empty sub-cubes, only gives poor speedups for datasets with a high percentage of occupied voxels. This is illustrated with the skull dataset where 88% of all voxels are occupied (see Table 7.1). A similar observation can be made for the foot dataset. Only for the fuel dataset performance gains of 280% can be observed which are due to the large areas of non-occupied voxels surrounding the compact union of occupied voxels.

Generally, much higher frame-rates can be achieved exploiting the given classification, resulting in performance gains ranging from 200% for the neghip dataset to 375% for the vessel dataset (additional to early ray termination). The performance gain for the neghip is only 200%, since a large number of samples still contribute to the final image. Overall, for the presented datasets of 256^3 voxels, we achieve frame-rates well above 15 frames per second.

While achieving good speed-ups additional to early ray termination, the selection of the appropriate sub-cube size is dataset and classification dependent. As a rule of thumb, a sub-cube size of 8^3 is suited for the smaller datasets (64^3)

and sub-cubes of 16^3 for the larger datasets (256^3), even though for a few cases slightly higher frame-rates can be achieved for the next smaller or larger sub-cube size.

The reported frame-rates will be even higher by skipping larger sub-cubes exploiting the given two-level hierarchy, as described in Section 7.1. In case all eight at even boundary addresses aligned neighboring sub-cubes are empty, a much larger distance can be skipped within a single cycle. Furthermore, for samples taken in empty sub-cubes, no memory request needs to be sent down the pipeline and hence, the overall memory efficiency will increase due to less page reloads. This is not yet incorporated in the numbers presented in Figure 7.3.2 and Table 7.3, since this requires a full simulation of the entire pipeline.

7.4 Summary

This chapter presented a new space leaping mechanism using an occupancy mask instead of an entire distance volume. With only $4Kbit$ of SRAM, it is able to significantly reduce the latency caused by reading distance volumes from the voxel memory. The latency due to the calculation of the new skipping value can be accommodated by processing eight rays, even in an FPGA design running at 100 MHz. The amount of extra logic required for the presented space leaping mechanism is less than 1% (130 CLBs) of an Xilinx Virtex XCV1000 FPGA.

Furthermore, using the VIZARDII system, the occupancy map can be classification dependent, since VIZARDII provides a sufficient memory bandwidth to update the occupancy map 50 times per second. Frame-rates well above 15 frames per second for datasets of 256^3 voxels were achieved, providing parallel and perspective projections, as well as arbitrary sampling rates in all three dimensions.

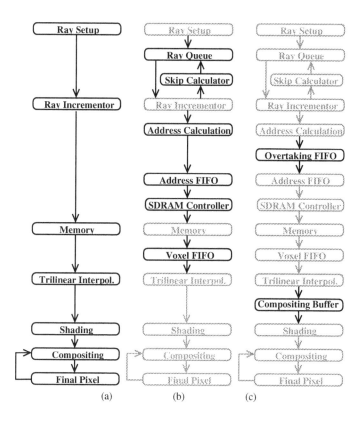

Figure 7.5: The stages in a ray casting pipeline. (a) Standard pipeline stages, (b) Extra units required for multiple rays and improved memory performance, (c) Further improving memory performance by sorting rays.

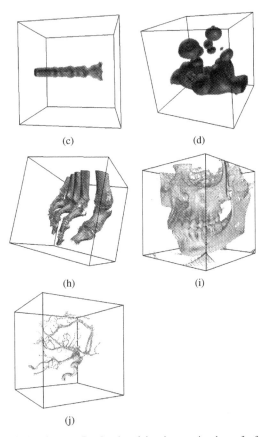

Figure 7.6: Test datasets: Rendered applying the associated transfer functions.

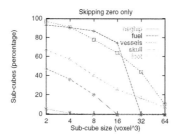

Figure 7.7: Percentage of skipable sub-cubes. Only empty voxels have been exploited.

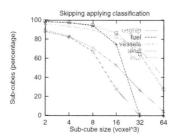

Figure 7.8: Percentage of skipable sub-cubes exploiting the given classification.

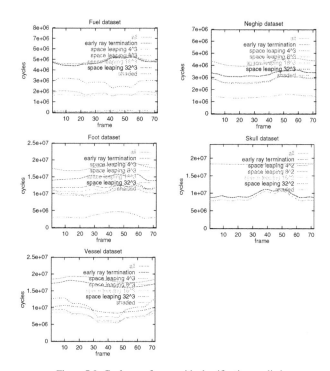

Figure 7.9: Cycles per frame, with classification applied.

Chapter 8

Ray Casting Antialiasing using Multiresolution Datasets

This chapter presents a solution to aliasing problems in ray casting driven volume rendering approaches and also uses sample frequency matching to improve interactive ray casting using multiresolution datasets. When perspective ray casting is used and a ray reaches a certain depth from the view plane, the distance between two rays can result in voxel data being missed by both rays. This missed data or undersampling can result in aliasing and can be solved using multiresolution datasets. Multiresolution datasets also allow the distance between sample points along a ray to be increased to match the density of data in lower resolutions of the dataset. This increase in the increment matches the sampling frequency to the density in the lower resolution datasets and offers some performance gain. The use of multiresolution voxel datasets introduces several problems including how to generate the lower resolutions of the dataset, when to switch between the resolutions of the dataset and how to classify newly calculated values that do not fit into the original dataset classifications. This chapter discusses these problems and presents results for several different datasets.

When perspective rendering is used for ray casting volume data and the distance between rays spans several voxels resulting in some voxels not contributing to the final image. Also when parallel projection is used the distance between rays can also span several voxels and result in the same undersampling problem. When the user rotates the object in an interactive system these voxels can appear to flash as they are intersected and missed by rays causing an aliasing effect. A solution to this aliasing effect using multiresolution datasets to ensure that no discrete data points at the original or lower resolutions are missed by rays is presented in the

105

following chapter.

The use of several levels of detail within a voxel dataset has been used previously for accelerating the rendering process in techniques such as octree based space leaping [55], hierarchical splatting [52], multiresolution Volume Rendering using a wavelet basis [86] and ray tracing of wavelet transforms [65]. While both octree space leaping and the sampling frequency matching presented in this chapter achieve the same effect, the concept behind when and how to implement these techniques are quite different. In contrast to [93] where multi-resolution rendering is performed dependent on the frequency in the dataset, we calculate multi-resolution based on the sampling of the current ray. Similarly, with hierarchical splatting and wavelet Volume Rendering, which aim to solve the more general problem of Volume Rendering, multiresolution datasets are used for ray casting approches in this chapter. Brady et al [6] propose an adaptive ray spawning scheme which increases the number of rays at step distances from the viewpoint to fulfil the sampling. Additionaly image compositing of the back segments over several frames in a sequence is used to improve performance. However the approach presented here does not generate new rays, but instead selects the appropriate volume resolution.

8.1 Multiresolution Datasets

A multiresolution dataset consists of the first level or level 0, which is the original data at full resolution and subsequent levels at a reduced resolution. Subsequent levels are taken at half the resolution of the previous level and only a few levels are usually required. Since the first level is $\frac{1}{8}$ the size of the first level the additional storage for multiresolution is minimal. For example, the sizes of levels in the CT head dataset used in Section 8.2.1 are $256 \times 256 \times 128$ for level 0, $128 \times 128 \times 64$ for level 1, $64 \times 64 \times 32$ for level 2 and $32 \times 32 \times 16$ for level 3. When using multiresolution datasets two interesting problems arise, firstly, how to calculate the lower resolutions, which is dealt with in Section 8.1.1, and secondly, at what point along a ray should data be taken from a higher level of the dataset, which is dealt with in Section 8.1.2.

8.1.1 Calculating lower resolutions

The most obvious way to calculate the next level in a multiresolution dataset is to take the average of the eight voxels that form a cube at the coordinates of the voxel to be calculated for the next level. In a region of mostly empty space the calculation of an average would produce empty space thereby eliminating any data, such as skin or bone, from the lower resolution. To a certain degree we would like to preserve small artifacts in the lower resolution so that at a distance they are still visible. To determine the best method for calculating the lower resolutions several methods were tested including: the median value; the average of voxels of interest only (i.e., skin, bone); an estimated marching cubes occupancy value; and an accurate marching cubes occupancy value. The marching cubes occupancy values were calculated using the 14 triangulated cubes presented by Lorensen[58]. First an estimated occupancy value for each of the 14 cases was calculated and then to calculate a lower resolution dataset each cube of 8 voxels was matched to one of 14 cubes and assigned the estimated value. To increase the accuracy each cube of 8 voxels was first matched to the correct case and then the vertices of the triangles inside the cube were calculated using linear interpolation of the adjacent voxels. Using these triangles the volume of occupied space was calculated within the cube and converted to a voxel value. The average of voxels of interest only and the accurate marching cubes occupancy value provided the best results. The problem with both of these methods is a slight growing effect on the dataset as discussed in Section 8.2.1.

Another problem with averaging the dataset is that a cube of voxels that might have several values belonging to one classification may have a resultant average that lies in another classification. In correctly segmented datasets the lower resolution value can be assigned the most correct segment or a new segment introduced. Without a segmented dataset the classification ranges may start to overlap requiring some sort of segmentation to be added.

Precomputed gradients, as used by VIZARDII presented in Chapter 9, can also be calculated at multiresolutions to improve the quality of the images rendered from lower resolutions.

8.1.2   Level switching

The main advantage of multiresolution datasets is the ability to avoid the aliasing visible when interactively rotating a dataset and applying insufficient sampling. Figure 8.1 shows two rays diverging and missing a voxel at sample 2. To ensure the voxel being missed is considered in sample and gradient calculation the lower resolution dataset is used.

This switching between the multiresolution dataset levels is shown in Figure 8.2. The distances shown in Figure 8.2 and the following equation are used to

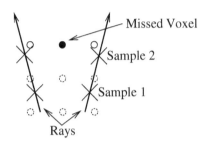

Figure 8.1: Rays missing a voxel when there are 3 voxels between them.

calculate the distance between two neighbouring rays:

$$V = D \times \frac{P}{S}$$ (8.1)

where,

<table>
<tr><td>V</td><td>is the distance between the current sample point and a sample point on a neighbouring ray,</td></tr>
<tr><td>D</td><td>is the distance from the viewpoint to the current sample point,</td></tr>
<tr><td>P</td><td>is the distance between the current pixel and a neighbouring pixel, and</td></tr>
<tr><td>S</td><td>is the distance from the viewpoint to the viewplane.</td></tr>
</table>

When V is greater than 2 then a voxel is usually missed so the next level in the dataset is used. Similarly, when level 1 is in use and the distance is again 2 voxels (measured in the level 1 resolution) then the next lower resolution of the dataset, level 2, is used. Measuring all distances in terms of level 0 voxels the switch to level 1 occurs when V is 2, level 2 when V is 4, level 3 when V is 8 and level n when V is 2^n. A distance of 3 or greater means that a voxel has been missed, but if switching was performed at a distance of 3 many voxels would be missed even at a distance of 2.

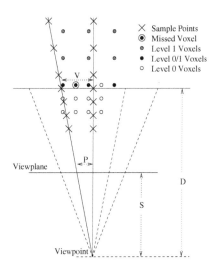

Figure 8.2: The distances used to calculate when to change resolutions in the multiresolution dataset.

8.2 Results

To demonstrate the impact of using multiresolution datasets, several datasets were rendered with and without lower resolutions.

Figure 8.3 shows three images generated from a dataset containing a 108^3 cube constructed from planes of voxels which start at the bottom with yellow, cyan, red and blue planes one voxel thick and are followed by subsequent groupings of the same colours. The cube is rotated 45 degrees to the viewing plane and only the bottom right quarter of the image is shown since the remainder of the image is a reflection of this corner. In Figure 8.3(a) the cube is close to the viewpoint and all rows of the cube are visible. The viewpoint is then moved away from the dataset and in Figure 8.3(a) and (b) we can clearly see aliasing of the rows. This aliasing is a result of undersampling the dataset and can be solved by switching to the lower resolution of the dataset as shown in Figure 8.3(c). Figure 8.3(c) introduces two new classifications to represent combinations of the original classifications. The new classifications are green for the combination of yellow and cyan and magenta for the combination of red and blue. These new classifications show how the problem of overlapping segmentation regions can be solved by introducing new segments.

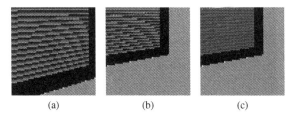

(a)   (b)   (c)

Figure 8.3: A voxel cube rendered without (a), (b) and with multiresolution (c).

Choosing colours that represent a combination of the colours used for the classification of the original resolution should provide a better visual result when changing between levels of the multiresolution dataset. To improve switching between the multiresolution levels further trilinear interpolation could be used similar to trilinear mipmapping as used for texture mapping[89].

8.2.1 Lower resolution datasets

Figure 8.4 shows several images of a skull taken from a $256 \times 256 \times 111$ Computed Tomography (CT) scan of a human head. The images in Figure 8.4 show the dataset at a distance of 80 voxels from the viewing plane and a resolution of 100×119 pixels. Figure 8.4 shows the dataset: rendered using only the original dataset (a), rendered using both the original dataset, level 0 and the next lower resolution level 1 (b), rendered with level 0 shown in grey and level 1 shown in red (c), and a difference image between Figures (a) and (b) in (d). The line left of the skull is removed by aliasing in image (a) but appears in the multiresolution images.

Figure 8.4(d) shows the growing effect that causes the object inside the dataset to increase in size at lower resolutions. This growing effect is a result of the algorithm used for multiresolution dataset generation and the classification of the dataset. This is a result of the voxels in the lower resolution being twice the size of the voxels in the higher resolution and since we want to preserve the structural information in the lower resolution this effect is difficult to eliminate. The effect can be prevented using different multiresolution dataset generation algorithms.

8.2.2 Sample frequency matching

Multiresolution datasets offer a speed improvement by matching the sampling frequency to data density in lower resolution datasets. The matching of the sampling frequency is shown in Figure 8.2 where the distance between samples is increased when a voxel is missed and the lower resolution dataset is used. Initial results for matching the sample frequency show speed ups of 70% for level 1, 88% for level 2 and 100% for level 3. The ray setup time and speedup from early ray termination have an increasing effect on the time taken to calculate a ray. For opaque classifications the resolution and sampling frequency are reduced resulting in marginal performance gains at lower multiresolution levels. While for highly transparent classifications much higher benefits are achieved.

The images in Figure 8.5 are rendered from a Confocal Microscopy dataset of a substance found inside a cell nucleus during a stage in the cell division process called pachytene and the dataset has a resolution of $512 \times 512 \times 64$ voxels. Figures 8.5(b), 8.5(c), and 8.5(d) are rendered using a sample increment value that is increased by a factor of two every time the level of the multiresolution dataset is changed. Figure 8.5(a) shows the original dataset rendered at 512×512 pixels. Figure 8.5(b) shows the dataset rendered at 925 voxels from the viewplane at a resolution of 259×259 pixels and shows level 0 in grey and level 1 in red. Figure 8.5(c) shows the dataset rendered at 2840 voxels from the viewplane at a resolution of 129×129 pixels and shows level 1 in red and level 2 in green. Figure 8.5(d) shows the dataset rendered at 6660 voxels from the viewplane at a resolution of 64×64 pixels and shows level 2 in green and level 3 in blue. Figures 8.5(b), (c) and (d) show that the switch between multiresolution levels and sampling frequency matching have little effect on the final image. In rendering all images in Figures 8.5 the increased increment speeds up the rendering accordingly and while the measured image difference is noticeable, the visual difference is less significant.

8.3 Summary

This chapter has presented techniques that use multiresolution datasets to correct the aliasing experienced in ray casting driven Volume Rendering systems and improve the performance by matching the sampling frequency to dataset density. These two techniques improve the image quality and offer a performance gain for Volume Rendering systems.

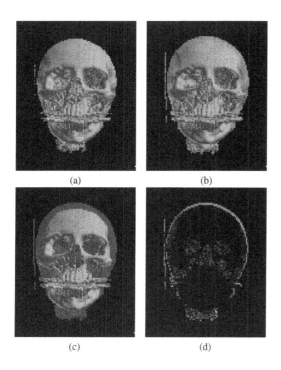

Figure 8.4: A CT dataset rendered (a) without and (b),(c) with multiresolution. (c) shows the second level in red and (d) is the difference between images (a) and (b).

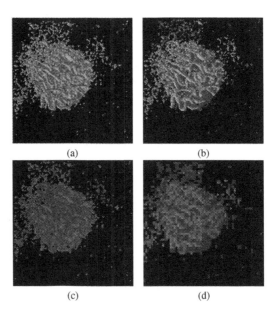

(a)   (b)

(c)   (d)

Figure 8.5: A Confocal Microscopy dataset rendered using matched sampling frequencies. (a) original, (b) level 0 grey and level 1 red (c) level 1 red and level 2 green, (d) level 2 green and level 3 blue.

Chapter 9

VIZARDII: A Programmable and Interactive Volume Rendering PCI Card

This chapter presents the VIZARDII Volume Rendering hardware accelerator for high quality perspective ray casting. VIZARDII performs ray casting by calculating the path of the ray through the volume using a programmable Xilinx Virtex FPGA which provides fast design changes and low cost development. Volume datasets are stored on the card in low profile DIMMs with standard connectors allowing both, large datasets up to 1 GByte with 32 bit per voxel, and easy upgrades to newer larger memory capacities. Per-sample post-classification and Phong shading is performed in hardware giving immediate feedback to changes in the visualization of a dataset. Adding new features can be done in a straight forward manner using the existing card without expensive and time consuming redesigns. The Card can also be used for Medical Image reconstruction by reconfiguring the FPGA broadening it's usefulness for end users. VIZARDII enables the generation of high quality photo and non-photo realistic perspective images as required for applications like virtual endoscopy and colonoscopy, and stereoscopic image generation.

This chapter describes the VIZARDII card, which is realized as a custom designed PCB with off-the-shelf components, as shown in Figure 9.1. VIZARDII generates images by casting rays into the dataset from the viewpoint instead of processing the dataset in its storage order. This is the major contrast to the VolumePro system[72] which must process every voxel in a volume dataset to generate an image. Image-order processing allows VIZARDII to generate perspective

115

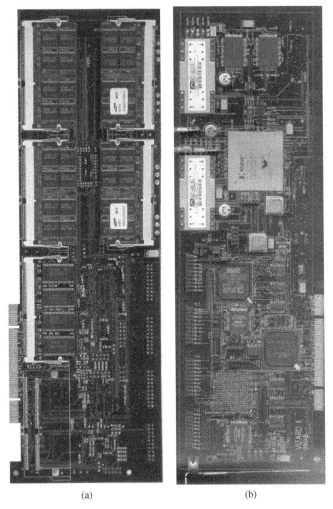

(a)   (b)

Figure 9.1: VIZARDII from below (a) and above (b).

images easily while taking advantage of optimization techniques such as early ray termination. The ability to customize the rendering process by reprogramming the FPGA for individual application areas further increases the possible uses of the system beyond previously available systems.

A true image-order algorithm is implemented, casting an individual ray for each pixel of the image. For each ray, the first sample location is determined by intersecting the ray and the volume or—in case the image plane intersects the volume—by taking the location on the image plane itself. Both, parallel and perspective projection are supported since they are both required for medical applications.

Sample values and gradients along the ray are generated using trilinear interpolation. We consider the gradient as a voxel property and store it together with the volume data. While this increases the memory requirements, it allows the use of different gradient operators, including higher quality gradient estimation schemes, such as the 3D Sobel operator. We discuss advantages of different gradient estimation schemes in Section 9.2.

Furthermore, non isotropic datasets, as frequently present when data originates from CT or MRI scanners, can easily be handled by distorting each component of the ray starting position and the ray increment by the respective volume spacing.

Classification is performed on the interpolated sample values and includes color (R,G,B), opacity(α), illumination parameters (k_a, k_d, k_s).

Illumination is done using Phong shading which is accomplished using two cube-maps, one for the diffuse shading intensity and one for the reflective intensity. The latter requires the computation of the reflected vector, following the work presented in [84]. Other techniques affecting the sample opacity are also enabled.

Values along a ray can either be accumulated following a discretization of the volume rendering line integral, or by performing Maximum Intensity Projection (MIP). The line integral accumulation is realized as front-to-back compositing, such that early ray termination can be exploited.

9.1   The Ray Processing Unit

The core of the system is the Ray Processing Unit (RPU). The RPU calculates color pixel values using the start position and increment values for a given ray. The architecture of the RPU is shown in Figure 9.2. The processing units—Raycaster, Address Calculation, Interpolation, Illumination, Classification, Combiner and Compositing—are outlined in black, the input and output data for each unit is

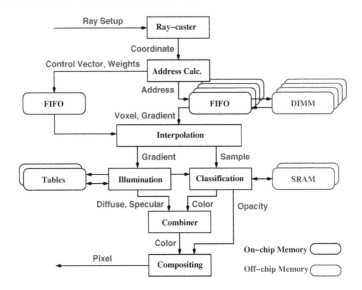

Figure 9.2: Architecture of the Ray Processing Unit (RPU).

indicated in green. The RPU uses on-chip memory for FIFOs and Lookup Tables. Volume data is stored in 4 DIMMs, with 256 MByte each, connected to the RPU. The Classification Tables are stored in two 32 bit wide SRAMs, with a capacity of 2 Mbit each.

9.1.1   Ray-caster

The Ray-caster traces rays through the volume, from a given ray entry position $\mathbf{P}_{entry} = P_x, P_y, P_z$, in the direction defined by the increment, $\mathbf{I} = I_x, I_y, I_z$, computing a new sample location every cycle. $\mathbf{P}_{entry}$ and $\mathbf{I}$ are calculated using floating point operations on a DSP and transferred to the Ray-caster in a fixed point representation. The ray increment has a 10 bit fractional part, allowing for arbitrary over-sampling. The coordinates of the current sample location are passed on to the Address Unit, along with a Control Vector indicating if the current sample is the first or last sample in it's ray. This control information is used by the Compositor to correctly start or terminate a ray. A ray is terminated when it exits the volume or the accumulated opacity in the Compositor exceeds a given threshold (Early Ray Termination).

The Compositor has to accumulate subsequent samples along a ray, such that the result of this operation is available in the next cycle. To achieve high image quality, this blending operation requires a 16-bit fixed point multiply-accumulate unit, that has to be pipelined in a high speed design—introducing more than one cycle of latency for the blending operations. This conflict can be overcome by casting multiple rays and interleaving the processing of these rays, as presented in Chapter 6, such that sample generation cycles over all rays before generating the subsequent sample along each individual ray.

A similar approach used to hide memory latency for distance volume based space leaping was presented in [82], but here we use fewer interleaved rays and do not sort sample positions. Casting four rays in parallel allows four cycles of latency for the actual compositing of the samples.

When using early ray termination, each ray in a group of four could be replaced immediately once it was terminated. However, this would result in a significant performance drop of the memory interface, due to the new ray being in a completely different part of memory. As more rays were terminated and added to the group of four this effect would worsen. Instead the entire group of four rays is only terminated once the opacity of all four rays passes a user defined threshold. We call this *Early Group Termination*.

Tracing multiple rays in parallel requires a ray number and a ray group number to be added to the Control Vector for each sample. The ray number is used by the Compositor to accumulate the current sample to the correct ray. The ray group number is sent back to the Ray-caster to indicate the ray group to be terminated when Early Group Termination occurs since the group being processed in the Compositor may not be the same as the one in the Ray-caster.

9.1.2 Address Calculation

An individual address for each of the DIMMs is calculated using the integer part of the current ray's sample position, using the address calculations presented in Section 9.3.1. The fractional part of the current ray position is used as the weighting factor in the tri-linear interpolation. To ensure correct timing for the Control Vector and the tri-linear interpolation weights, these values pass through a FIFO while the voxel values are read from the volume memory.

9.1.3   Interpolation

A total of four tri-linear interpolations needs to be performed (sample and gradient components), making this the largest of all units. The tri-linear interpolation is implemented as three stages of linear interpolations. While re-phrasing the linear interpolation (Equation 9.1) saves one multiplier (Equation 9.2), the multiplication can be performed using only positive values by swapping a and b if $b > a$.

$$c = a(1-w) + bw \tag{9.1}$$
$$c = a - w(a - b) \tag{9.2}$$

The swapping is already needed due to the memory interleaving where the values alternate depending on odd and even X, Y coordinate access values. When the inputs need to be swapped, a bit is set in the Control Vector for X and Y interpolation.

9.1.4   Illumination

Illumination is typically calculated using a surface normal which must be normalized using a square root calculation. The implementation of this is costly, non trivial, and still requires the evaluation of the illumination model. Given the constraints on available logic and a reasonable amount of on-chip SRAM, we used two cube-maps to calculate view point independent Phong shading as presented in [84]. Reflection vector shading hardware[84] improves the visual appearance by using a per pixel calculated reflection vector (which doesn't need to be normalised) to look up into a cube environment map to generate specular highlights at texturing speed, independent of the number of light sources. The diffuse cube-map uses the gradient at the current sample point to calculate which face of the six faces of a cube-map to access and then calculates the four addresses required to access one face of the cube-map. The cube-map data is stored in an interleaved fashion as shown in Figure 9.3, so that the four neighboring values can be accessed in a single cycle, allowing a bilinear interpolation in each cycle. The calculation of the specular component requires the reflection vector to be calculated from the eye point and then the reflection vector is used to access the cube-map containing the specular component.

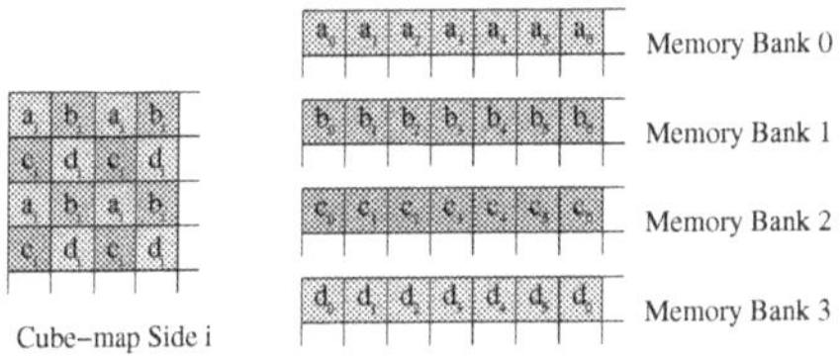

Figure 9.3: The interleaving of the entries of one face of the cube-map to ensure four values are read in one cycle.

9.1.5 Classification

The Classification unit reads the $R, G, B, \alpha, k_a, k_d$, and k_s from the SRAMs, using the current sample value as an index. Each of these values are 8 bit wide, except the opacity value (α) which has 16 bit to ensure high precision. In case Maximum Intensity Projection (MIP) is enabled, no color classification is performed, but the original sample value is simply forwarded.

9.1.6 Combiner

In case shading is enabled, the final color value for the sample point is calculated by combining the values of the Classification unit with the intensities from the Illumination unit, using the following equation:

$$C = k_a I_a + k_d I_d Color + k_s I_s, \qquad (9.3)$$

where k_a, k_d and k_s are material properties for the current sample, I_a, I_d, and I_s are the ambient, diffuse, and specular intensities from the Illumination unit, and *Color* is the color value read from the classification table for the current sample value. If shading is disabled, the color values are simply forwarded.

9.1.7 Compositing

The output of the Combiner is a stream of color and opacity values in a front to back order for the current group of rays. Either the highest sample value along each ray is stored (Maximum Intensity Projection (MIP)) or the values are accumulated along their respective rays:

$$C_{n+1} = C_n + C_{sample} \alpha_{sample} (1 - \alpha_n) \qquad (9.4)$$

$$\alpha_{n+1} = \alpha_n + \alpha_{sample} (1 - \alpha_n) \qquad (9.5)$$

The accumulated color values as well as the accumulated opacity are 16 bit values, ensuring high quality images even for low opacity samples.

Additionally, the Compositing unit compares the current opacity value to a user defined opacity threshold. In case this threshold is reached for all four interleaved rays, an early ray termination signal is sent to the Ray-caster which then starts a new group of rays in case the terminated group of rays is still being processed[1]. A nice side-effect of interleaving multiple rays is the increased efficiency of early ray termination since the latency of the pipeline is distributed over four rays reducing the overall latency costs per ray. Generally, early ray termination has a significant effect on performance for inside views of datasets such as colonoscopy and for viewing a volume datasets with many opaque objects. An advantage of image-order approaches is that early ray termination can be integrated easily while it is hard to exploit in object-order algorithms.

9.2 Complex Gradient Filters

High quality gradient estimation is critical for volume rendering, not only for illumination but also for boundary enhancement using gradient magnitude modulation. While simple gradient filters can be computed on the fly by designing the memory interface appropriately, complex and high-quality gradient filters put a burden on the memory interface and can not be accomplished at reasonable cost. In order to enable different gradient estimation schemes, we consider the gradient a voxel property as the normal is a vertex property in surface graphics. Thus, it is stored together with actual volume data and allows any gradient filter to be used[2].

---

[1]This is tested by checking a ray-group Id which is part of the control vector and sent together with the early ray termination signal.

[2]While the gradient computation is a pre-processing step, it can be computed on the FPGA on the fly while downloading the dataset into the DIMM modules.

9.3 Voxel Memory

The voxel memory must meet the size and performance requirements of modern Volume Rendering without pushing the cost beyond the realm of standard PC class machines. With higher modality resolutions becoming increasingly common place, large volume datasets, up to 1 GByte in size with voxel widths of up to 32 bit, are supported. The memory interface presented in Chapter 5 is used in order to provide the image-order ray casting algorithm with virtually random access to voxel memory while at the same time reducing the stalling effects caused by SDRAM memory. The basic concepts of the memory interface are presented in Chapter 5 so only the implementation details used for VIZARDII are presented in the following.

9.3.1 Sub-cube Memory Organization

The DIMMs allow for $16 \times 8 \times 8$ voxels to be stored in each row. Combining the four interleaved DIMMs, this results in a sub-cube size of 16^3. A 64^3 dataset thus contains 4^3 sub-cubes. The address values for the four DIMMs are calculated using the current sample, taking into account the sub-cube and interleaved memory organization. For a given coordinate $C_{x,y,z}$, the four DIMM addresses $A_{D0...D3}$ are computed by first calculating the address for the current sub-cube (SC) and the relative address within the sub-cube (RA):

$$SC = (\frac{C_z}{16} \cdot SubC_X \cdot SubC_Y) + (\frac{C_y}{8} \cdot SubC_X) + \frac{C_x}{8} \quad (9.6)$$
$$RA = 64(C_z \bmod 16) + 8(C_y \bmod 8) + C_x \bmod 8 \quad (9.7)$$

where $SubC_{X,Y}$ is the number of sub-cubes in the X, Y Dimensions respectively. The final address is then obtained using the following formula:

$$A_{D0...D3} = SC \cdot SubC_S + RA \quad (9.8)$$

where the sub-cube size $SubC_S = 8 \times 8 \times 16 = 1024$ represents the number of voxels in each sub-cube, which is stored in an SDRAM row. To account for the interleaving of the memory in the X and Y dimensions, the coordinate $C_{x,y,z}$, used to calculate each individual DIMM address, is modified from the current sample coordinate, $P_{x,y,z}$, according to the DIMMs relative position using the following formulas:

$$\text{DIMM 0: } C_{x,y,z} = (\frac{P_x}{2} + P_x \text{ mod } 2, \frac{P_y}{2} + P_y \text{ mod } 2, P_z) \tag{9.9}$$

$$\text{DIMM 1: } C_{x,y,z} = (P_x, \frac{P_y}{2} + P_y \text{ mod } 2, P_z) \tag{9.10}$$

$$\text{DIMM 2: } C_{x,y,z} = (\frac{P_x}{2} + P_x \text{ mod } 2, P_y, P_z) \tag{9.11}$$

$$\text{DIMM 3: } C_{x,y,z} = (P_x, P_y, P_z) \tag{9.12}$$

$$\tag{9.13}$$

9.4   VIZARDII PCI Card

The PCI Card is a custom Printed Circuit Board design, using off-the-shelf components. Figure 9.4 shows an overview of the card architecture. The local bus,

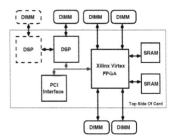

Figure 9.4: Architecture of the PCI Card. The main data and address bus is shown in red and the optional DSP and DIMM are shown using dashed lines.

connecting the PCI Interface, DSP and Virtex, shown in red, is used to transfer data into and out of the Virtex, memories and DSP via the PCI Interface. The PCI Interface Chip[3], DSPs[4], Virtex FPGA and SRAMs are located on the top side of

---

[3]PLX Technologies PCI 9054 ASIC.

[4]When configured for medical image reconstruction the board also uses a second DSP and associated DIMM (shown in Figure 9.4 with dashed lines) which is not required for Volume Rendering.

the board (marked by a box in Figure 9.4) while the bottom side of the board holds up to six low profile DIMMs.

Two power converters have been added on the top side of the board to supply additional power for the board components, since the PCI Bus cannot supply enough power for all DIMMs.

9.4.1 DSP

The Digital Signal Processor (DSP) is a SHARC ADSP-21160, responsible for ray setup calculations and local bus arbitration on the PCI card. The ray setup consists of calculating the entry point into the volume (P_{entry}) and the increment (I) for each ray. The entry point is calculated using a modified version of a ray-box intersection algorithm presented by Woo[91]. The exit point of the volume is not required since the Ray-caster checks the current sample position of the ray against volume minimum and maximum values.

9.4.2 Xilinx Virtex FPGA

The Xilinx Virtex FPGA (XCV2000E Fine Grid 680 Package) contains the main processing units (RPU, memory interfaces, FIFOs and required control logic). It is connected to four DIMMs for storing the volume dataset and two SRAMs for storing classification tables. The top level architecture of the Virtex is shown in Figure 9.5.

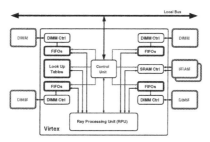

Figure 9.5: Architecture of the Xilinx Virtex FPGA. The data download buses are indicated in Green.

FIFOs, attached to each DIMM memory controller, are used to improve memory performance as explained in Chapter 5. An additional memory controller is required for the two SRAMs, which contain the Classification Tables. The Look Up Tables are stored in on-chip BlockRAM which is dual ported, allowing simultaneous data loading and reading. The RPU accepts ray entry and increment values and returns a completed pixel value for each ray to the Control Unit.

9.4.3   Control Unit

The Control Unit is responsible for the downloading of data, setup for rendering and control of the rendering process. Control is handled through a series of commands issued from the software interface and passed through to the Virtex by the DSP. An Instruction Decoder inside the Control Unit interprets and maintains control of the Virtex based on these passed instructions. Data required for the Volume Rendering pipeline must be downloaded via the Virtex to appropriate memory modules including: volume data to the DIMMs; Classification Tables to the SRAMs; Look Up Tables to the Virtex BlockRAMs; rendering and dataset setup data for the RPU; and individual ray data for the Ray-caster in the RPU. Incoming ray data and outgoing pixel values are both buffered by the Control Unit in case the local bus is busy.

9.4.4   Logic Usage and Layout

The rendering engine implemented on a Xilinx Virtex FPGA occupies 6015 CLBs (Configurable Logic Blocks)[5]. FIFOs and Look Up Tables are implemented using 42 Virtex BlockRAMs [38], each 4Kbit large, resulting in a total of 21.5 KBytes of SRAM storage.

Figure 9.6 depicts the layout on the FPGA. About one third of the resources are used by the Interpolation unit, due to the 28 multipliers used. In Figure 9.6 Control logic is colored magenta, the Ray-caster blue, the Interpolation unit green, the Illumination unit yellow, the Combiner red, and the Compositing unit cyan.

---

[5]A CLB consists of four SRAM based lookup tables to implement combinatorial logic, four storage elements configurable as D-flip-flops or latches, and dedicated carry and control logic [38].

Figure 9.6: Colored Floorplan of the Virtex FPGA.

9.4.5 Rendering Performance

There are a multitude of factors that affect the frame-rate performance of the PCI Card. Image size dictates the number of rays traced and sampling rate determines the number of samples processed by the pipeline. Generally, a peak performance of a 100 Mega samples can be achieved. With a more effective usage of the samples, like early ray termination or spaceleaping, the possible frame-rates can be improved even more. Therefore with a single ray casting pipeline, we accomplish real-time frame-rates for most datasets. Examples of the images generated by the VIZARDII system are shown in Figure 9.7. Figure 9.7(a) is Virtual Endoscopy, (b) a lobster with extreme perspective, (c) a close-up of an aneurism, and (d) a rendering of an Engine Block. The ventrical fly-through shown in Figure 9.7(a) is rendered at 20-30 frames per second for a image sizes of 256^2.

9.5 Summary

This chapter presented the algorithms and architecture used for the VIZARDII interactive Volume Rendering PCI Card. In particular high quality perspective images with a fully interactively controllable feature set is presented for the first time. The feature set includes: 32 bit voxel representation, pre-computed gradients, per-sample Phong shading, α-blending with 16 bit precision, and non-isotropic datasets. VIZARDII is targeted at the field of Volume Visualization which includes a wide variety of applications with a very large set of feature requirements. The use of an FPGA means that the board can be easily reprogrammed when new features are required. This allows for the board to be reconfigured and retargeted

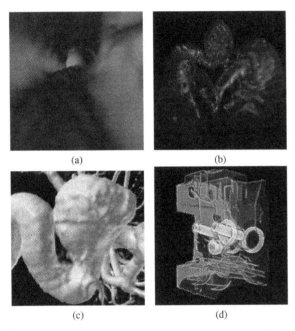

(a)   (b)

(c)   (d)

Figure 9.7: Images generated by VIZARDII showing (a) a ventricle fly-through, (b) a lobster, (c) an aneurism and (d) a transparent engine block.

at other markets including the reconstruction of medical images from medical imaging modalities[6].

While the VolumePro[72] system offers more frames per second based on a higher number of samples per second, VIZARDII processes fewer more relevant samples at a lower sample processing rate to produce higher quality perspective images. This accelerator uses the first uncompromized, yet still optimized, implementation of the ray casting algorithm allowing for a new level of flexibility and algorithmic optimizations previously unseen in Volume Rendering hardware accelerators. Also programmability, more accurate image generation through high accuracy gradients, applications such as Virtual Endoscopy, Virtual Colonscopy and others where stereoscopic viewing is required are all possible.

The reprogrammability of the VIZARDII PCI Card will allow for future exploration of many interesting research directions. This includes the space leaping presented in Chapter 7, multiresolution datasets as presented in Chapter 8, and even the Displacement mapping architectures in Chapters 4 and 3. Further directions also include the mixing of polygons with volumetric datasets, multiple rendering pipelines, and splatting [87] based Volume Rendering. By upgrading the FPGA chip as ever increasing numbers of gates become available on newer FPGA chips work has already started on new features such as gradient magnitude modulation and non-photo realistic rendering using using the existing board but a larger FPGA chip. The low-cost, reprogrammability, arbitrary ray projection and sampling of VIZARDII are an improvement over all previous interactive Volume Rendering solutions in terms of high quality interactive rendering that we hope will give end-users greater insight into Volume data.

---

[6]The board when outfitted and reconfigured for reconstruction is being used by an international medical imaging systems company.

Bibliography

[1] John Amanatides and Andrew Woo. A fast voxel traversal algorithm for ray tracing. In *EuroGraphics*, pages 1–10, August 1987.

[2] Marga Amor, Montse Boo, Michael Doggett, Johannes Hirche, and Wolfgang Strasser. A meshing scheme for memory efficient adaptive rendering of subdivision surfaces. Technical Report WSI-2000-21, Wilhelm Schickard Institute for Computer Science, Graphical-Interactive Systems (WSI/GRIS), University of Tübingen, 2000.

[3] ATI. RADEONVolVis, Volume Visualization on the RADEON. Software and details available from http://www.ati.com, 2000.

[4] I. Bitter and A. Kaufman. A ray-slice-sweep volume rendering engine. In *Proceedings of the 1997 EUROGRAPHICS/SIGGRAPH Hardware Workshop*, Los Angeles, CA, 1997.

[5] Jim Blinn. *Jim Blinn's Corner: A Trip down the graphics pipeline.* Morgan Kaufmann, 1996. Chapter 17: Hyperbolic Interpolation.

[6] Martin L. Brady, Kenneth K. Jung, H. T. Nguyen, and Thinh PQ Nguyen. Interactive volume navigation. *IEEE Transactions on Visualization and Computer Graphics*, 4(3):243–256, July-September 1998. ISSN 1077-2626.

[7] D. E. Breen, S. Mauch, and R. T. Whitaker. 3D Scan Conversion of CSG Models into Distance Volumes. In *Symposium on Volume Visualization*, pages 7–14, Research Triangle Park, NC, October 1998.

[8] B. Cabral, N. Cam, and J. Foran. Accelerated Volume Rendering and Tomographic Reconstruction Using Texture Mapping Hardware. In *Workshop on Volume Visualization*, pages 91–98, Washington, DC, October 1994.

[9] Daniel Cohen and Amit Shaked. Photo-realistic imaging of digital terrains. In *Eurographics '93*, pages 363–373, 1993.

[10] Robert L. Cook. Shade Trees. *Computer Graphics (Proceedings of SIG-GRAPH 84)*, 18(3):223–231, July 1984. Held in Minneapolis, Minnesota.

[11] Franklin C. Crow. Summed-Area Tables for Texture Mapping. *Computer Graphics (Proceedings of SIGGRAPH 84)*, 18(3):207–212, July 1984. Held in Minneapolis, Minnesota.

[12] T. J. Cullip and U. Neumann. Accelerating Volume Reconstruction with 3D Texture Mapping Hardware. Technical Report TR93-027, Department of Computer Science at the University of North Carolina, Chapel Hill, 1993.

[13] M de Boer, A Gröpl, J Hesser, and R Männer. Latency and hazard-free volume memory architecture for direct volume rendering. In *Eurographics Workshop on Graphics Hardware*, pages 109–119, August 1996.

[14] Michael Doggett. An array based design for real-time volume rendering. In *Eurographics Workshop on Graphics Hardware*, pages 93–101. EuroGraphics, August 1995.

[15] Michael Doggett. A Ray Queueing and Sorting Design for Real Time Ray Casting. In *International Symposium on Circuits and Systems*. IEEE, May 2000.

[16] Michael Doggett and Johannes Hirche. Adaptive view dependent tessellation of displacement maps. In *SIGGRAPH/Eurographics Workshop on Graphics Hardware*, pages 59–66, August 2000.

[17] Michael Doggett and Johannes Hirche. Displacement mapping rendering hardware using adaptive tessellation. presented at ACM SIGGRAPH 2000 as a Technical Sketch, July 2000.

[18] Michael Doggett and Anders Kugler. A Hardware Architecture for Displacement Mapping using Scan Conversion. Technical Report WSI–99–12, Wilhelm-Schickard-Institut für Informatik, University of Tübingen, Germany, 1999.

[19] Michael Doggett, Anders Kugler, and Wolfgang Straßer. Displacement Mapping using Scan Conversion Hardware Architectures. *Computer Graphics Forum*, To appear in 2001.

[20] Michael Doggett and Michael Meißner. A memory addressing and access design for real time volume rendering. In *International Symposium on Circuits and Systems*. IEEE, May 1999.

[21] Michael Doggett, Michael Meißner, and Urs Kanus. A Low-Cost memory architecture for PCI-Based Interactive Ray Casting. In *Eurographics/SIGGRAPH Workshop on Graphics Hardware*, pages 7–14, August 1999.

[22] Michael Doggett and Michael Meißner. Ray casting : Antialiasing using multiresolution datasets. In *Informatik 2000: Graphikta*, september 2000.

[23] Michael C. Doggett. *VIZAR: A Video Rate System for Volume Visualization*. PhD thesis, School of Computer Science and Engineering, University of New South Wales, August 1996.

[24] Michael C. Doggett and Graham R. Hellestrand. A hardware architecture for video rate smooth shading of volume data. *Computers and Graphics*, 19(5):695–704, September 1995.

[25] I. Ernst, D. Jackél, H. Rüsseler, and O. Wittig. Hardware-supported bump mapping. *Computers and Graphics*, 20(4):515–521, 1996.

[26] Jon P. Ewins, Marcus D. Waller, Martin White, and Paul F. Lister. Mip-map level selection for texture mapping. *IEEE Transactions on Visualization and Computer Graphics*, 4(4):317–329, October 1998.

[27] Kurt Fleischer and David Salesin. *Graphics Gems III*, chapter VII.6 Accurate polygon scan conversion using half-open intervals, pages 362–365. Academic Press, 1992.

[28] M. Flynn. On division by funcional iteration. *IEEE Transactions on Computers*, 19(8):702–706, 1970.

[29] James D. Foley, Andries van Dam, Steven K. Feiner, and John F. Hughes. *Computer Graphics: Principles and Practice*. Addison Wesley, 1989.

[30] Michael Garland and Paul S. Heckbert. Fast polygonal approximation of terrains and height fields. Technical Report CMU-CS-95-181, Carnegie Mellon University, 1995.

[31] S. Gibson. Using Distance Maps for Accurate Surface Representation in Sampled Volumes. In *Symposium on Volume Visualization*, pages 23–30, Research Triangle Park, NC, October 1998.

[32] Stefan Gumhold and Tobias Hüttner. Multiresolution rendering with displacement mapping. In *Eurographics/SIGGRAPH Workshop on Graphics Hardware*, pages 55–66, August 1999.

[33] T. Günther, C. Poliwoda, C. Reinhart, J. Hesser, R. Männer, H.-P. Meinzer, and H.-J. Baur. VIRIM: A massively parallel processor for real-time volume visualization in medicine. In *Eurographics workshop on Graphics Hardware*, pages 103–108, September 1994.

[34] Paul S. Heckbert. Survey of texture mapping. *IEEE Computer Graphics and Applications*, 6(11):56–67, 1986.

[35] Paul S. Heckbert and Henry P. Moreton. Interpolation for polygon texture mapping and shading. In *State of the Art in Computer Graphics: Visualization and Modeling*, pages 101–111. Springer-Verlag, 1991.

[36] Wolfgang Heidrich. *High-quality Shading and Lighting for Hardware-accelerated Rendering*. PhD thesis, Der Technischen Fakultät der Universität Erlangen-Nürnberg, 1999.

[37] W. M. Hsu. Segmented ray-casting for data parallel volume rendering. In *Proceedings of the 1993 Parallel Rendering Symposium*, pages 7–14, San Jose, CA, 1993.

[38] Xilinx Inc. Virtex-E 1.8 V Field Programmable Gate Arrays. Preliminary Product Specification, available from http://www.xilinx.com/, 2000.

[39] D. Jackel. The graphics parcum system: A 3d memory based computer architecture for processing and display of solid models. *Computer Graphics Forum*, 4(1):21–32, 1985.

[40] U. Kanus, M. Meißner, W. Straßer, H. Pfister, A. Kaufman, R. Amerson, R. J. Carter, B. Culbertson, P. Kuekes, and G. Snider. Implementations of Cube-4 on the teramac custom computing machine. *Computers & Graphics*, 21(2):199–208, 1997.

[41] Arie Kaufman and Reuven Bakalash. Memory and processing architecture for 3D voxel-based imagery. *IEEE Computer Graphics and Applications*, 8(11):10–23, November 1988.

[42] Mark J. Kilgard. A Practical and Robust Bump-Mapping Technique for Today's GPUs. Technical report, NVIDIA Corporation, www.nvidia.com, February 2000.

[43] R. Klein, A. Schilling, and W. Straßer. Reconstruction and simplification of surfaces from contours. In Bob Werner, editor, *Proc. of the Seventh Pacific Conference on Computer Graphics and Applications*, pages 198–207, Seoul, Korea, October 1999.

[44] Günter Knittel. VERVE : Voxel Engine for Real-time Visualization and Examination. *Computer Graphics Forum*, 12(3):37–48, 1993.

[45] Günter Knittel. A PCI-based volume rendering accelerator. In *Eurographics Workshop on Graphics Hardware*, pages 73–82, August 1995.

[46] Günter Knittel and Wolfgang Straßer. VIZARD: Visualization accelerator for realtime display. In *1997 Eurographics/SIGGRAPH Workshop on Graphics Hardware*, pages 139–147, August 1997.

[47] K. Kreeger and A. Kaufman. PAVLOV: A Programmable Architecture for Volume Processing. In *Proc. of Eurographics/SIGGRAPH workshop on graphics hardware 1998*, pages 77–86, Lisboa, Portugal, 1998.

[48] Venkat Krishnamurthy and Marc Levoy. Fitting smooth surfaces to dense polygon meshes. *Proceedings of SIGGRAPH 96*, pages 313–324, August 1996. ISBN 0-201-94800-1. Held in New Orleans, Louisiana.

[49] Anders Kugler. The setup for triangle rasterization. In *Eurographics/SIGGRAPH Workshop on Graphics Hardware*, pages 49–58, August 1996.

[50] Anders Kugler. IMEM: an intelligent memory for bump- and reflection-mapping. In *Eurographics/SIGGRAPH Workshop on Graphics Hardware*, pages 113–122, August 1998.

[51] Philippe Lacroute and Marc Levoy. Fast volume rendering using a shear-warp factorization of the viewing transformation. In *Computer Graphics*, pages 451–458. ACM SIGGRAPH, July 1994.

[52] E. Laur and P. Hanrahan. Hierarchical splatting: A progressive refinement algorithm for volume rendering. In *Computer Graphics, Proc. of SIGGRAPH 91*, pages 285–288. ACM, 1991.

[53] Aaron Lee, Henry Moreton, and Hugues Hoppe. Displaced subdivision surfaces. In *Computer Graphics, Proc. of SIGGRAPH 2000*. ACM, 2000.

[54] Marc Levoy. Display of surfaces from volume data. *IEEE Computer Graphics and Applications*, 8(5):29–37, May 1988.

[55] Marc Levoy. Efficient ray tracing of volume data. *ACM Transactions on Graphics*, 9(3), July 1990.

[56] B. Lichtenbelt. Design of a high performance volume visualization system. In *Proceedings of the 1997 Eurographics/SIGGRAPH Hardware Workshop*, Los Angeles, CA, 1997.

[57] J. Lichtermann. Design of a fast voxel processor for parallel volume visualization. In *Proceedings of the 10th Eurographics Hardware Workshop*, pages 83–92, Maastricht, The Netherlands, 1995.

[58] William Lorensen and Harvey Cline. Marching Cubes: a high resolution 3D surface construction algorithm. In *Computer Graphics, Proc. of SIGGRAPH 87*, pages 163–169. ACM, 1987.

[59] K. Ma, J. Painter, C. Hansen, and M. Krogh. A Data Distributed Parallel Algorithm for Ray-Traced Volume Rendering. In *Proceedings of IEEE Symposium on Parallel Rendering*, pages 15–22. ACM Press, October 1993.

[60] Joel McCormack, Robert McNamara, Christopher Gianos, Larry Seiler, Norman P. Jouppi, Ken Correl, Todd Dutton, and John Zurawski. Neon: A (Big) (Fast) Single-Chip 3D Workstation Graphics Accelerator. Research Report 98/1, COMPAQ WRL, 1999.

[61] Joel McCormack, Robert McNamara, Christopher Gianos, Larry Seiler, Norman P. Jouppi, and Ken Correll. Neon: A single-chip 3d workstation graphics accelerator. In *Eurographics/SIGGRAPH Workshop on Graphics Hardware*, pages 123–132, August 1998.

[62] Michael Meißner, Michael Doggett, Urs Kanus, and Johannes Hirche. Accelerating volume rendering using an on-chip sram occupancy map. In *International Symposium on Circuits and Systems*, Sydney, Australia, May To appear in 2001. IEEE.

[63] Michael Meißner, Urs Kanus, and Wolfgang Straßer. VIZARD II, A PCI-Card for Real-Time Volume Rendering. In *Eurographics/SIGGRAPH Workshop on Graphics Hardware*, pages 61–67, August 1998.

[64] Kazunori Miyata. A method of generating stone wall patterns. In *Computer Graphics, Proc. of SIGGRAPH 90*, pages 387–394. ACM, 1990.

[65] Shigeru Muraki. Volume data and wavelet transform. *IEEE Computer Graphics & Applications*, 13(4):50–56, July 1993.

[66] NEC, http://www.necel.com. *μPD45256163 256M-bit Synchronous DRAM*, 1998.

[67] Michael Meißner, Ulrich Hoffmann, and Wolfgang Straßer. Enabling Classification and Shading for 3D Texture Mapping based Volume Rendering using OpenGL and Extensions. In *Visualization*. IEEE, 1999.

[68] U. Neumann. Parallel volume-rendering algorithm performance on mesh-connected multicomputers. In *1993 Parallel Rendering Symposium Proceedings*, pages 97–104, San Jose, CA, October 1993.

[69] Randy Osborne, Hanspeter Pfister, Hugh Lauer, Neil McKenzie, Sarah Gibson, Wally Hiatt, and TakaHide Ohkami. EM-Cube: an architecture for low-cost real-time volume rendering. In *Eurographics/SIGGRAPH Workshop on Graphics Hardware*, pages 131–138, August 1997.

[70] Hans Køhling Pedersen. Displacement mapping using flow fields. In *Computer Graphics, Proc. of SIGGRAPH 94*, pages 279–286. ACM, 1994.

[71] Mark Peercy, John Airey, and Brian Cabral. Efficient bump mapping hardware. In *Computer Graphics, Proc. of SIGGRAPH 97*, pages 303–306. ACM, 1997.

[72] Hanspeter Pfister, Jan Hardenbergh, Jim Knittel, Hugh Lauer, and Larry Seiler. The volumepro real-time ray-casting system. In *Computer Graphics, Proc. of SIGGRAPH 99*, pages 251–260. ACM, 1999.

[73] Hanspeter Pfister and Arie E. Kaufman. Cube-4 - A scalable architecture for real-time volume rendering. In *1996 Volume Visualization Symposium*, pages 47–54. IEEE, October 1996.

[74] Matt Pharr and Pat Hanrahan. Geometry caching for ray-tracing displacement maps. In *Eurographics Workshop on Rendering*, June 1996.

[75] H. Ray and D. Silver. A Memory Efficient Architecture for Real-Time Parallel and Perspective Direct Volume Rendering. Technical Report CAIP-TR-237, Department of Computer Aids for Industrial Productivity, Rutgers University, 1999.

[76] C. Rezk-Salama, K. Engel, M. Bauer, G. Greiner, and T. Ertl. Interactive Volume Rendering on Standard PC Graphics Hardware Using Multi-Textures and Multi-Stage Rasterization. In *Eurographics/SIGGRAPH Workshop on Graphics Hardware*, August 2000.

[77] Alyn P. Rockwood, Kurt Heaton, and Tom Davis. Real-time rendering of trimmed surfaces. *Computer Graphics (Proceedings of SIGGRAPH 89)*, 23(3):107–116, July 1989. Held in Boston, Massachusetts.

[78] Gernot Schaufler and Markus Priglinger. Efficient displacement mapping by image warping. In *Eurographics Workshop on Rendering*, 1999.

[79] Andreas Schilling. Towards real-time photorealistic rendering: Challenges and solutions. In *Eurographics/SIGGRAPH Workshop on Graphics Hardware*, pages 7–15, August 1997.

[80] Johnathan Shade, Steven Gortler, Li wei He, and Richard Szeliski. Layered depth images. In *Computer Graphics, Proc. of SIGGRAPH 98*, pages 231–242. ACM, 1998.

[81] M. Sramek. Fast Surface Rendering from Raster Data by Voxel Traversal Using Chessboard Distance. In *Proc. of IEEE Visualization*, pages 188–195, Washington, D.C., October 1994.

[82] B. Vettermann, J. Hesser, and R. Männer. Solving the hazard problem for algorithmically optimized real-time volume rendering. In *International Workshop on Volume Graphics*, March 1999.

[83] Alex Vlachos, Jörg Peters, Chas Boyd, and Jason L. Mitchell. Curved PN Triangles. In *Symposium on Interactive 3D Graphics*. ACM, March 2001.

[84] Douglas Voorhies and Jim Foran. Reflection vector shading hardware. In *Computer Graphics, Proc. of SIGGRAPH 94*, pages 163–166. ACM, 1994.

[85] R. Westermann and T. Ertl. Efficiently using graphics hardware in volume rendering applications. *Proceedings of SIGGRAPH 98*, pages 169–178, July 1998.

[86] Rüdiger Westermann. A multiresolution framework for volume rendering. In *Symposium on Volume Visualization*, pages 51–58, October 1994.

[87] L. Westover. Footprint Evaluation for Volume Rendering. In *Computer Graphics*, Proc. of ACM SIGGRAPH, pages 367–376, August 1990.

[88] Martin White, Mike Bassett, Dairsie Latimer, Shaun McCann, Alex Makris, Marcus Waller, Graham Dunnett, Joachim Binder, and Paul Lister. The TAYRA 3-D graphics raster processor. *Computers & Graphics*, 21(2):129–142, March 1997.

[89] Lance Williams. Pyramidal Parametrics. In *Computer Graphics, Proc. of SIGGRAPH 83*. ACM, 1983.

[90] Andrew Witkin and Michael Kass. Reaction-diffusion textures. In Thomas W. Sederberg, editor, *Computer Graphics (SIGGRAPH '91 Proceedings)*, volume 25, pages 299–308, July 1991.

[91] A. Woo. *Graphics Gems*, chapter Fast Ray-Box Intersection, pages 395–396. Academic Press, Inc., 1990.

[92] Mason Woo, Jackie Neider, and Tom Davis. *OpenGL Programming Guide*. Addison Wesley, 1997.

[93] Yuting Yang, Feng Lin, and Hock Soon Seah. Fast Multi-Resolution Volume Rendering. In *International Workshop on Volume Graphics*, pages 49–64, 1999.

[94] K. Z. Zuiderveld, A. H. J. Koning, and M. A. Viergever. Acceleration of ray catsing using 3D distance transform. In R. A. Robb, editor, *Proc. of Visualization in Biomedical Computing*, pages 324–335, Chapel Hill, NC, October 1992. SPIE, Vol. 1808.

www.ingramcontent.com/pod-product-compliance
Lightning Source LLC
Chambersburg PA
CBHW031548080326
40690CB00054B/715